PEOPLE OF THE PASSION

Stephen C Barton is Lecturer in New Testament
in the Department of Theology of the University
of Durham. He is also a non-stipendiary minister
at St John's Church Neville's Cross, Durham.
Previously he taught at Bishop Otter College,
Chichester Theological College and Salisbury
and Wells Theological College. He is a member
of the Church of England Board for Social
Responsibility Working Party on the Family. His
first book was *The Spirituality of the Gospels*
(SPCK 1992).

F44/01

PEOPLE
of the
PASSION

Stephen C Barton

TRiANGLE

First published 1994
Triangle
SPCK
Holy Trinity Church
Marylebone Road
London NW1 4DU

British Library Cataloguing in Publication Data
A catalogue record for this book is available from the British Library
ISBN 0–281–04729–4

Typeset by Inforum, Rowlands Castle, Hants
Printed in Great Britain by
BPCC Paperbacks Ltd
Aylesbury, Bucks
Member of BPCC Ltd

CONTENTS

To
Roger and Margaret Crane
and their two sons
Stephen and Jonathan

PREFACE

This book is based on a series of Bible studies made possible by an invitation from the Dean and Chapter of Durham Cathedral to give a course of lunchtime lectures for Lent 1993, the year of the 900th anniversary of the founding of the cathedral. It is a pleasure now to express my thanks to my colleague David Brown, whose idea it was, and to Margaret Parker who did the organizational work and hosted the meetings. She it was also who suggested the theme for the lectures, which has become the title of the book: *People of the Passion*.

The lectures were written during a busy Lent Term in the Theology Department of Durham University. They were also part of my training at Cranmer Hall for the nonstipendiary ministry of the Church of England, so I have many people in both places to thank. In the Department, I received particular help from Walter Moberly at the initial stage of discussing ideas and texts, and from Ann Loades and Peter Selby who read the lectures through and commented very helpfully on them. In Cranmer Hall, I was given great encouragement by the Warden, John Pritchard, and by Ivy George, a visiting lecturer in sociology. The audience at the lectures, made up of people from both the cathedral congregation and the local churches, was very encouraging also, and I am grateful to them for their support. Warm thanks are due also to Rachel Boulding and her colleagues at SPCK for their help in turning the original lectures into a book. The Hepburn family of High Mickley provided again the hospitality which enabled a smooth rewriting of the manuscript. My wife

Fiona, together with our children, Anna, Thomas, Joseph and Miriam, provide, as ever, the kind of day-to-day support and *joie de vivre* which have made this work possible.

It is a privilege, finally, to dedicate this book to Roger and Margaret Crane, and to their sons, Stephen (my godson) and Jonathan, who live in the country town of Westbrook in Queensland, Australia, my own country of origin. The book is small recompense for their faithful friendship over the years and for their hospitality to me for three memorable days in January 1993.

Stephen C Barton
Department of Theology
University of Durham

1 The Strange Economy of Love

The Woman who Anoints Jesus

(Mark 14.3–9)

When I was a theology student, one of my teachers once said to the class I was attending, 'The most important lesson in learning to read the Bible well is learning to be surprised.' It was a curious thing to say, and I suppose that is why I remembered it. What he was getting at was that the more familiar we are with a story or text, the more likely we are to assume that we know already what it is saying, an assumption which gets in the way of our learning something new or seeing in the story something we have not seen before.

For Christians, Lent can be a time for seeing things that perhaps we have not seen before. It is a time for giving things up, letting things go and taking time out. If we do these things it may happen that, by travelling a little lighter, we may be led along new paths of faith and understanding in our discipleship of Christ and in our worship of God. So it is a good time to learn to be surprised. And if we can do that, we are on the road already to being open to change and to letting God's Spirit renew our lives.

The Bible is a book full of surprises. That is one reason why, down through the ages, reading the Bible has been a constant source of inspiration, guidance and provocation

1

to people of faith who have wanted to discern more clearly what God is like and how God is to be worshipped and obeyed. If that is true of the Bible as a whole, it is true also of the little stories within that bigger story. For Christians observing Lent, Holy Week and Easter, it is true above all of the passion of Christ. In the faith of the Church, it is *that* story which stands at the very heart of things and reveals that God himself is very much a 'God of surprises' who has lots of surprises in store – and not always welcome ones! – for those willing to trust in him.

So we turn first to the account of the passion in Mark's Gospel, and in particular, to the remarkable story in Mark 14.3–9 of the woman who anoints Jesus. I have chosen this episode for a number of reasons.

First, it is important to Mark. If we compare John's version (see John 12.1–8), we find that the anointing comes six days before the Passover and before Jesus enters Jerusalem so it is not part of John's passion narrative proper. In Mark, on the other hand, it is set at the beginning of his account of the passion. Here, it is two days before the Passover, and the entry into Jerusalem has happened earlier on (Mark 11.1–11). So it must be of particular significance to Mark, not least because it propels the story forward by telling us what it was that finally drove Judas to betray his master to the chief priests (14.10–11).

It is also important because it is the story of a woman – a woman whose action for Jesus has given her an indelible place in Christian memory. Professor Cranfield's 1963 commentary on Mark simply says: 'That it was a woman who anointed him is interesting.'[1] But he does not elaborate. Today, at a time in the life of our Church and society when we are more aware than ever before of prejudice against women and of the tendency to make women 'invis-

2

ible', we need to go further than this. We need to point out, for example, that Jesus does not speak of any other character in the Gospel, not even a Peter or a James or a John, in the glowing terms he uses of this woman: 'Truly I tell you: wherever the gospel is proclaimed throughout the world, what she has done will be told as her memorial' (v.9). Lent is a time for preaching the gospel of Christ and meditating upon it. So it is a time for remembering this woman and allowing her story to speak to us.

The other reason why this story is important is because it expresses the gospel in a nutshell. It is about an ordinary person who could be you or me expressing her love for Christ by an act of open, spontaneous generosity towards him. The action generates hostility and misunderstanding from those around her who should have known better. But from Christ himself her reward is to be fully accepted as a true witness to his coming death: 'she has anointed my body in anticipation of my burial' (v.8). The woman, in other words, is a model disciple and her story vividly expresses what Mark's Gospel as a whole is trying to say. As Jesus puts it in Mark 8.35, in 'losing her life' for his sake, she has saved it. Lent, too, is about losing our lives for Christ's sake, which is why the story of the anointing woman is a story for us as well.

There are a number of things that rank as surprising in the details of the story. There is the time and place: 'It was two days before the festival of Passover and Unleavened Bread' (14.1). Here, on the eve of the most solemn of Jewish festivals, the time of Passover, when the Jews celebrate God setting them free from their captivity to Pharaoh in Egypt, something very perverse and tragic is going on. The leaders of the people, who should have known better, are seeking to arrest and kill Jesus, the one who has come to deliver Israel from a more powerful form of captivity, Israel's captivity to Satan. What is more, they are seeking to do this 'by deceit'. The word 'deceit' occurs also in Jesus's list of defiling things in 7.21–22. This suggests that the chief priests and scribes are impure at the very time (Passover) when purity is most demanded of them. What they are doing is perverse and essentially self-serving. They want to do away with Jesus privately in order to avoid a public disturbance (v.2).

The woman is different. Her action in anointing Jesus with the 'pure oil of nard' is surely more in the spirit of the feast. Where the leading men plot murder, the woman expresses love. Where the leading men operate privately and in a premeditated way by stealth, the woman acts openly and without regard for the consequences. Where their acts are self-serving, she performs a service for someone other than herself. The account of how the leaders behave is shot through with elements which are the reverse of what we expect of them. This kind of reversal has to do with the setting of the episode as well. In Jerusalem, the city of God, the chief priests of God's holy place plot their Messiah's death. In Bethany, in a leper's house (v.3) – that is, a place regarded by the people of the time as ritually impure – a woman performs an act of purity and grace.

Who acts more in the spirit of the feast? This is not an artificial question but one which springs naturally from the very heart of our story. It is also a question which we can address to ourselves as readers and hearers of the story. This Lent, Holy Week and Easter, are we acting in the spirit of the feast? Are we, like the chief priests and scribes, doing what is self-serving and death-dealing in the way we live and in the kind of society we build? Or are we, like the woman, doing what is loving and life-giving? The challenge is simple and direct, and invites our response.

People who are genuinely religious and who give themselves to faithful observance of the festivals of the Christian calendar, are often at risk of losing the connection between liturgy and life. We cease to understand liturgy as the offering to God of our everyday lives, and we lose the sense of our daily lives as the outworking of what we say and do in a more concentrated, symbolic way in the liturgy. The two parts of our lives drift apart and become only loosely connected. Putting it in terms of our weekly routine, Sunday – the Christian 'sabbath' – becomes the fag-end of a week consumed by work and worry; it degenerates into a kind of ritual escape or afterthought, instead of being the first day of the week, the day whose rest and celebration establish the life-giving basis for the six days to come.

So this story presents us with a challenge. It is a challenge to act in the spirit of the feast: to let the liturgies of Easter flow over into the 'liturgies' of everyday life. Just as the Jewish Passover is a celebration of God setting his people free from the bonds of slavery in Egypt, and just as Easter is a celebration of God-in-Christ freeing people from the bonds of slavery to sin, so we ourselves are invited to live as God's free people. We are called to acts of liberality which help set others free.

Now for the second surprise. Even though the story ends with Jesus lavishly praising the woman by saying that 'wherever the gospel is proclaimed throughout the whole world, what she has done will be told as her memorial' (v.9), we are not told of her name! The woman is and remains anonymous, at least so far as the Gospel of Mark is concerned.

What is the effect of her anonymity? There are two effects, I think. On the one hand, the fact that she is anonymous places her alongside other anonymous characters in

Mark, all of whom are exemplary in some way and many of whom are women. There is Simon Peter's mother-in-law, the woman with the haemorrhage, the daughter of Jairus, the Syro-Phoenician woman and her unnamed daughter, the mothers who bring their children to Jesus for his blessing, and the 'many women' who followed Jesus from Galilee and were present at the crucifixion. Among anonymous characters who are men, there is the man possessed by demons, the leper, the man with the withered hand, the deaf mute, and the centurion at the cross.

It is as if Mark is helping us to see that the gospel is both *for* ordinary people and *about* ordinary people – women as well as men, outsiders as well as insiders, people at the margins as well as people at the centre, children as well as grown-ups. In other words, you don't need any special qualifications to be a follower of Jesus and to belong to the people of God. Sex, rank, status, property, health, occupation, where you live – all of them so important in the traditional agrarian society of Jesus's day, as well as in traditional societies generally – no longer matter in the same way. These factors do not somehow lose their significance and disappear. But they no longer have quite the *same* significance. This comes through clearly in a saying of Jesus earlier in Mark's narrative when people coming to him had been given a hostile reception by the disciples. 'Let the children come to me, do not hinder them,' says Jesus, 'for to such belongs the kingdom of God' (10.14). The gospel is for those whom we might call the 'little people', and it is those 'little people' who show us what the gospel is about. Here it is an anonymous woman. In a previous episode, not unrelated to this one, it is a 'poor widow' (12.42).

The other effect of the woman's anonymity, together with the anonymity of her accusers (14.4–5), is that it invites us as readers or hearers of the story to identify ourselves with one or other of the two parties. As I said earlier, the episode invites us to see ourselves in the characters and in the conflict, to see our own story in the light of the woman's story. This provides us with a marvellous, life-transforming opportunity. Very often, we think of ourselves as people who do not matter very much, people whom life has left behind, people with no 'name'. Yet Mark's Gospel is full of stories of people with no name, like this one about the woman who anoints Jesus. And they are the people to whom Jesus comes with words of grace and healing. They are the people too who appear most able to respond wholeheartedly and without reservation.

Another surprise also has to do with the woman. It is the fact that she does not say one word in the entire episode, despite the provocation she receives! Clearly, the focus of the story is on *what she does*. It is a case of actions speaking louder than words. And Jesus backs this up. He silences the angry objectors and defends the woman, a defence which draws attention three times to the woman's action: 'It is a fine thing she has done for me' (literally, 'She has worked a good work upon me', v.6); 'She has done what lay in her power' (v.8); and '. . . what she has done will be told as her memorial' (v.9).

Why this emphasis on what the woman has done? It is partly because what you do expresses far more clearly than words whose side you are on and where your heart really lies. We are reminded of Saint Paul: 'I may speak in tongues of men or of angels, but if I have no love, I am a sounding gong or a clanging cymbal' (1 Corinthians 13.1). And Jesus said something similar in the Sermon on the Mount: 'Not everyone who says to me, "Lord, Lord", will enter the kingdom of Heaven, but only those who do the will of my heavenly Father' (Matthew 7.21). But it is a major theme in Mark, as well. It comes up much earlier in the Gospel, when Jesus's mother and brothers come 'seeking' Jesus. When Jesus is informed that his kinsfolk are 'outside', he replies, very deliberately looking around at the crowd sitting about him: 'Here are my mother and my brothers! Whoever does the will of God is my brother and sister and mother' (3.33–34). This shows that to belong to Jesus's family requires doing the will of God. And although only his mother and brothers come seeking him, Jesus speaks of a different kind of family which includes 'sisters' also. This links in well with our story of the woman who anoints Jesus. She acts boldly on behalf of Jesus, and in so doing, shows herself to be a 'sister' to him. Contrast Peter, the leading disciple. In his case, there are lots of words, even good, 'correct' words: 'Even if I have to die with you, I will never disown you' (see 14.27–31). But when it comes to the crunch, Peter denies his Lord three times.

The focus on the woman's action also shows that she is awake to the moment of opportunity presented by the presence of Jesus in Simon's house. Here is her chance to express in unambiguous terms her devotion to Christ. Here is her moment of truth and she will not let it pass her by. It is as if she is aware already that Jesus's days are numbered. As Jesus says himself: 'you will not always have me' (v.7). So she must act, and she must act now for time is short. In doing so, she shows herself yet again to be a model disciple. It is no coincidence that in the long speech of Jesus about the events of the end time – a speech which immediately precedes our story – the constant refrain is about the need to be on guard, to keep awake, and to watch for the sudden coming of the Son of Man (13.3–37).

8

This is what the woman does, she has kept awake for the coming of Jesus into her life. This is in marked contrast to the twelve male disciples who, in the Garden of Gethsemane, all fall asleep and subsequently run away (14.32–50).

But her action is exemplary for yet another reason. It demonstrates what I would like to call *the strange economy of love*. I refer to it this way because what she does is so *wasteful*! Twice we are told how valuable the ointment is: it is 'very costly' (v.3); and it is worth more than three hundred denarii (v.5), where (according to Matthew 20.2) a denarius is a day's wage for a labourer. Her action is also wasteful in breaking the bottle containing the ointment, for now it can never be used again (v.3). So her action does not make economic sense. But maybe that is the point! Perhaps the economy of love works along different lines. For according to the economy of love, the appropriate way to behave is not a matter of mere financial calculation: it demands passionate and total self-giving in response to the moment of opportunity which the presence of Jesus provides.

The obligation of giving to the poor is not denied (v.7). On the contrary, it is affirmed by Jesus himself. But giving money to the poor is no substitute for acts of love and devotion which spring from and witness to a different kind of 'economy' altogether – the economy of the kingdom of God. For Christians, it is that 'uneconomic' economy of the kingdom which underpins and inspires the practice of giving to the poor. You cannot have the one without the other.

This woman is not the only witness in Mark to the strange economy of love. There is another woman whose actions are described a little earlier, in 12.41–44, just before the Mount of Olives discourse. She too does not speak a word. Instead, this 'poor widow' comes to the treasury in the temple and puts in 'two tiny coins, together worth a penny' (v.42). Now this does not make economic sense either. On the one hand, a penny is such a trifle that it is worthless economically. On the other hand, the money she contributes to the treasury is the only money she has left, for according to the watching Jesus, 'she, with less than enough, has given all that she had to live on' (v.44). Clearly, economic sense is not the point. The point is the strange economy of love. It is also saying that true worship of God and true discipleship of Jesus do not come on the cheap. Such devotion will cost the disciple his or her life, just as it cost Jesus his. The basic principle is set out earlier in the Gospel, after Jesus's first prediction of his death: 'Anyone who wants to be a follower of mine must re-nounce self; he must take up his cross and follow me. Whoever wants to save his life will lose it, but whoever loses his life for my sake and for the gospel's will save it' (8.34–35). This is one of Jesus's most important 'whoever' statements. It is addressed to you and me and to every reader and hearer of the Gospel.

The final surprise has to do with the words of Jesus in defence of the woman (vv.6–9). I have in mind especially the second part of his response: 'She has done what lay in her power; she has anointed my body in anticipation of my burial' (v.8). Now, it is important to note that Jesus has the last word in this story. What he says is the climax, and it ends with an emphatic, 'Truly I tell you . . .' kind of saying. So we can be sure that Mark wants the words of Jesus to be the authoritative comment on the whole episode.

My question is, since the woman does not say anything, how does Jesus know that her action in pouring the oint-ment over his *head* is intended as an anointing of his *body* in anticipation of his burial? The short answer, I think, is that he does not know her intentions, but chooses nevertheless to *interpret* her action in this way, as pointing forward to his death. And it is because Jesus interprets her action like this that her story becomes bound up inextricably with his, with the result that whenever the gospel of Christ crucified is preached, her story is remembered as well.

Jesus's inspired interpretation of the woman's action conflicts with the way in which Simon's other table companions (who probably include the twelve disciples) understand it. They see her action only in very mundane, financial terms, as if it is only the money and everyday responsibilities that matter. Jesus sees her action in *evangelical* terms – that is, as an expression of the gospel. Whether or not the woman had this in mind when she came with the bottle of perfume is not disclosed. What matters is that Jesus provides a *way of seeing* her action which is not a distortion of what she may have had in mind, but which gives it a deeper meaning and lifts her into the heart of the gospel. That is the woman's reward. Her sacrifice for Jesus's sake wins her a place in Christian memory and gospel preaching. Where the companions interpret her action in a way which threatens to strangle the life out of what she has done, Jesus offers an interpretation which *opens up* the woman's action and makes it part of a wider, divinely ordained action.

Lent is a traditional time for fasting. Yet this episode in Jesus's passion, and the others which we will go on to look at, provide sumptuous food for thought – and, of course, not for thought only.

This opening chapter has been a reminder of the importance of memory and the act of remembrance. This is one of the ways we shape ourselves as Christian people and as the Christian Church – through individual and shared acts of remembrance. And the story we have been looking at reminds us that ordinary people are a central part of Christian memory as well as extraordinary people. Or perhaps we should say, rather, that according to Mark, the ordinary people *are* the extraordinary people. The story reminds us also that women are a central part of Christian memory as well as men. Hence the very last words of the story: 'as *her* memorial'. We need, still, in many of our most important social and ecclesiastical institutions, to take that lesson to heart.

The story also speaks to us of the importance of doing what we can in the present moment and the present situation. Often, we prefer the much more romantic (and self-deceiving) option of trying to do the impossible. But Jesus commends the woman because she did 'what lay in her power' (v.8). On the one hand, she is not daunted by the possibility of doing something when the moment presents itself. But on the other hand, she does not overreach herself. She does the possible in the time available. Nor is it too far-fetched, perhaps, to interpret her action as a kind of grieving, since Jesus says, 'she has anointed my body in anticipation of my burial' (v.8). However that may be, there is wisdom and a challenge here: to do for God and for our neighbour what lies already within our power, and to confront the pride and self-protectiveness which holds us back from doing anything for fear that we cannot do everything.

Finally, we are alerted to the need to be awake to the moments of opportunity which God provides for us to show where our hearts really lie and whose side we are really on. This means action, not just talk: action which may look silly or which might be controversial, but which is not done for controversy's sake. On the contrary, what we are shown here is the importance of acts of devotion to Christ which spring from the strange economy of love, as expressed pre-eminently in the passion of Christ himself. It is the extravagance and the apparent waste which are so controversial. But it is precisely that which makes the deepest impact, even on Jesus himself. It allows him to see in a new light what the woman has done: as expressing the extravagant love of God and the wasteful way of the cross.

This wastefulness, this prodigality at the heart of the story is something which, if we let it, can break the mould in the way we live and in the way we relate to God and to one another. Here there is no calculation about what I or we will get out of it. There is just joy in giving and being given to. There is too an acceptance that life is more than what can be measured in financial or political terms. Perhaps this is where Judas's blind spot lies, for now he acts to hand Jesus over to the authorities (see vv.10–11). And this ominous development in the story raises the question as to how much we can be like Judas when we turn our backs on the prodigality at the heart of God. The woman, however, shows us a different way.

2 Love's Expense

Judas

(Matthew 27.3–10)

We turn in our second meditation on people of the passion, from the luminous story of the woman who anoints Jesus in demonstration of her love, to the very dark story of Judas. This is a natural progression. It matches the sequence in Mark and Matthew, where the story of the anointing is followed immediately by the decisive act of betrayal, when Judas – as if propelled by the event of the anointing in Simon's house – goes to the chief priests in order to betray Jesus to them (Mark 14.10–11; Matthew 26.14–16).

But we are going to have to struggle. Understanding what the story of Judas might be about is not going to be easy. We do not like staring the dark side of human nature in the face, because we are not often very well equipped to attend to the dark side even of ourselves. We want to find a scapegoat instead. We need to have someone else or something else to blame, a trait that has been with us from the time of Adam's complaint about Eve to God in the garden (Genesis 3.12). This is a reason for observing Lent. It is a time for being in the wilderness, a time for going out into the desert ourselves instead of sending out the scapegoat, a time for wrestling with God and being tested by the devil. It is a time for dealing with the Judas in you and the Judas in me.

We will not be the first, however, to have struggled over Judas. Will not Jesus himself have struggled over Judas, one of the twelve, one whom he had chosen to be with him, and yet who he knew would betray him (John 13.21)? And how else are we to explain the rents and gaps and noisy silences in the Gospel accounts of Judas unless we think of the problem Judas must have constituted for the early Church's understanding of itself and witness to others?

Mark is strikingly reticent about Judas. He mentions him by name only three times in all – once in 3.19, when Jesus chooses the twelve, and twice in the passion narrative at the end of the Gospel (14.10, 43). He gives no reason why the anointing by the woman should precipitate Judas's act of betrayal (14.10–11). And, after the arrest in Gethsemane (14.43–52), we hear nothing further of him. If, in Mark, the main mystery is the one which surrounds the identity of Jesus the Son of Man, there is also a mystery surrounding Judas.

Matthew is more helpful, but not necessarily more profound. For Matthew, Judas's motive in the betrayal is greed: ' "What will you give me to betray him to you?" They weighed him out thirty pieces of silver.' (26.15). And it is Matthew alone of the Gospel writers who satisfies our curiosity about the fate of Judas (as well as of the pieces of silver) by passing on an account of Judas's suicide (27.3–10). The account must have been important to Matthew, for it constitutes his most extensive addition to the basic framework of the passion narrative that he has taken over from Mark. We will come back to it later.

Luke treats Judas somewhat more sympathetically. Judas is a victim, not so much of avarice as in Matthew (though note Acts 1.18), but of Satan. The story of the wasteful anointing, which seems to precipitate the betrayal in Mark and Matthew, is absent (see 7.36–50). Instead, Luke says abruptly, 'Then Satan entered into Judas, who was called Iscariot, one of the Twelve' (22.3). Indeed, Luke is unique among the synoptic writers in the prominence he gives to Satan's presence during the passion, for Simon Peter is also depicted as a victim of satanic attack, though in his case, he is protected by Jesus's prayers on his behalf (22.31–32). It is also interesting that Luke does not have Jesus say of Judas, 'It would be better for that man if he had never been born' (22.22 – contrast Mark 14.21; Matthew 26.24). And, when it comes to the arrest in the garden, it looks as though Jesus actually prevents Judas from giving the betrayer's kiss (Luke 22.47–48)! There is an account of Judas's fate, but it is reserved for the early part of Luke's second volume where the story of finding a replacement apostle is told (Acts 1.15–26). And here we have, not suicide by hanging (as in Matthew), but divine judgment of the Ananias and Sapphira kind (Acts 5.1–11): 'this man fell headlong [presumably from the roof of the house he has just bought with his ill-gotten gains] and burst open so that all his entrails spilled out' (Acts 1.18).

Then there is the Judas of the Gospel of John. Here, the portrait is darkest of all. While according to Luke Judas becomes a victim of satanic possession, in John he becomes demonic. The very first time he is mentioned by name, Jesus is represented as saying, 'Have I not chosen the twelve of you? Yet one of you is a devil' (6.70). In John's account of the anointing at Bethany, the ones who object to the waste are now identified; and it is no longer a 'they' but a 'he' – it is Judas Iscariot (12.4–5). Furthermore, Judas's question there about almsgiving is supplied with a motive showing his wickedness: 'He [Judas] said this, not out of any concern for the poor, but because he was a thief; he had charge of the common purse and used to pilfer the money kept in it' (12.6). A thief and a man inspired by the devil: John's portrait takes up elements already in the traditions about Judas and develops them more fully. Jesus washes the disciples' feet, but Judas remains unclean (13.10–11). Jesus is the light of the world, but Judas is a creature of the night (13.30). And it is in the night that he comes with the forces of darkness – the Roman soldiers and the officers from the chief priests and the Pharisees – to take captive the Light of the World (18.1–12). That is the last we hear of him. As in Mark's account, his story is left disturbingly open.

But it is time now for us to struggle with Judas, and to see how Judas and the stories about him might speak to us this Lent.

The first point of struggle must be this: why does Jesus choose Judas as one of the twelve if he knows from the beginning that Judas will betray him? In the synoptic Gospel accounts of the choosing of the twelve, it is all very deliberate. In Mark, Jesus goes to a special place of revelation, a mountain, and 'summoned the men he wanted' (Mark 3.13); and the last of the twelve whom Jesus chooses so deliberately to be one of his companions (3.14) is Judas Iscariot, 'the man who betrayed him' (3.19). In Luke, the premeditation is just as strong, if not stronger, since Jesus is portrayed as spending the whole night before choosing the twelve 'in prayer to God' (Luke 6.12–13). Once again, Judas is identified explicitly as the one 'who turned traitor' (6.16). In John's Gospel, there is no corresponding account of the calling of the twelve: it is rather taken for granted. All the more striking, then, is the fact that when Jesus refers specifically to the disciples whom he has called, he pinpoints Judas and identifies him explicitly as a devil (John 6.70). So we can hardly say that Jesus does not know what he is doing in choosing Judas, and that the betrayal comes as a surprise. On the contrary, all four Gospel writers want their readers to understand that Jesus deliberately chooses as a member of his intimate circle of twelve someone who will betray him.

Our simple question must be, *why?* Different kinds of answers are possible, but the most helpful will be those which are most in the spirit of the Gospels themselves and of the gospel in which Christians believe. So I do not think an adequate answer would be that Jesus has some kind of 'death wish' for which Judas is the necessary instrument. Jesus's prayer in Gethsemane – 'Abba, Father, . . . take this cup from me' (Mark 14.36) – rules out any possibility that he wanted to die. And the idea of Judas as merely the passive instrument of forces greater than himself is a fatalistic position which is not in the spirit of the Gospels. If Judas is an instrument of forces greater than himself, there is no indication that he makes any attempt to resist those forces. On the contrary, he co-operates with them. The account of the suicide in Matthew (27.3–10) shows clearly that Judas accepts responsibility for what he has done.

A more adequate answer is that the Gospel accounts express something important about the nature of true friendship: that friendship entails *risk*, and that Jesus, by entering into partnership with twelve fallible followers, one of whom will betray him, another of whom will deny him, and all of whom will desert him, is himself willing to take that risk no matter what. It may be significant that when Judas comes with the soldiers to arrest Jesus, according to Matthew, Jesus calls Judas, 'friend' (26.50). But why are these friendships so important? Presumably because Jesus knows that not even he can go it alone. He knows too that the kingdom of God he proclaims has to be embodied in relations between ordinary, weak human beings, and that others will be needed to continue the work he is beginning. So Jesus does not cut himself off in self-protective isolation, but gathers around himself a group of friends and co-workers, though the risk is mortal.

To put it another way, it is a matter of treasure in earthen vessels. The community which Jesus brings into being and which becomes the Church is made up of followers who are fallible through and through; there will even be those who will defect and threaten the most serious harm. But the risk and the vulnerability has to be accepted, otherwise there can be no true love and no progress to maturity. That is the way of Jesus, so it must be the way of the Church as well.

But maybe there is more to it still. Perhaps, in choosing one who is demonic as a member of his intimate group, Jesus is embracing the darkness and incorporating it into himself – *not* in order to flirt with the darkness, of course, but in order to know it and, in knowing it, to overcome it. Such a picture is a powerful one. It means that Jesus's enemies are not just those in the other camp – whether the demonic world, the Herodians, the Pharisees, the chief priests, or the Roman authorities – but people who inhabit his own. So the testing and the temptation are not confined to a single encounter in the desert at the beginning of his mission, but are part of his daily intercourse with his companions. In terms of the famous metaphor from Paul, Judas is for Jesus his 'thorn in the flesh' (2 Corinthians 12.7). Such testing goes all the way to the cross. On the cross, Jesus embraces the darkness one last time and, by dying, absorbs the darkness into himself, thereby overcoming it. That is what Christians mean when they speak of the *atonement*: God, in the person of his Son Jesus, embraces the darkness and overcomes it once and for all on the cross. Perhaps, then, the choosing of Judas by Jesus is a kind of parable. For God's love is like that. God chooses, and gives his life for, even those who will betray him. That is *love's expense*.

If our first difficulty with Judas has been to do with why Jesus chooses one who will betray him, the second puts the question from the other side – why does Judas betray Jesus? What can be his motive, if he has one? After all, Jesus chooses him to be one of the twelve and to have the honour of sharing with him in the mission to Israel, as well as being a privileged witness to so much of what Jesus says and does. Peter's speech about Judas in Acts 1 sets out clearly Judas's apostolic credentials and authority: 'he was one of our number, and had his place in this ministry' (Acts 1.17). And when Peter comes to pray about the choice of a successor to Judas, he says that the one chosen is 'to receive this office of ministry and apostleship which Judas abandoned' (1.25). So Judas has this position of intimacy and status which derives from his association with Jesus. He even shares with Jesus and the eleven in the last supper (Luke 22.14–23; John 13.2–30). That he should become a traitor seems inexplicable.

As we have seen already – but need now to take further – the evangelists open up a variety of possibilities by way of explanation. We need to consider these, not so much for the insight they might give us into the psychology of Judas or the psychology of the Gospel writers, as for how they might speak about God, the world and the human condition to disciples of Jesus today.

First, there is greed. That is hinted at in Mark ('they promised him money', 14.11) and Luke (22.5; and Acts 1.18). But in Matthew, the motif of greed bulks large; for when Judas goes to the chief priests, he asks quite forthrightly, ' "What will you give me to betray him to you?" '

And the narrator says, 'They weighed him out thirty silver pieces. From that moment he began to look for an opportunity to betray him' (26.15–16). There is a warning here. Matthew is saying that even the most intimate relations of loyalty and trust can be blighted by greed. Somehow, Judas's love of money comes to take the place of his love of Jesus to the point where the two loves become incompatible and the one destroys the other. And, of course, Jesus himself has taught precisely this in the Sermon on the Mount: 'Do not store up for yourselves treasure on earth, where moth and rust destroy, and thieves break in and steal; but store up treasure in heaven . . . For where your treasure is, there will your heart be also . . . You cannot serve God and Money' (Matthew 6.19–21, 24).

The New Testament scholar Bertil Gärtner wants to play down the motif of greed in the interpretation of Judas. He is concerned that the story of Judas should not be reduced to cheap moralizing. And he explains the obvious presence of the motif of greed in this way: 'It is possible that it was an attempt to give a simple and rational answer to a naïve question: how was it possible that one of the twelve disciples acted so incomprehensibly and betrayed Jesus? By emphasizing that he was a thief, one solved the problem in a satisfying way. For a reader of the gospel it was not so easy to grasp and understand the theologically more complicated conception of the place of Judas in salvation history.'[1] Nevertheless, while it is important not to reduce the Judas story to moralizing about greed, it is important also not to avoid staring in the face the fact of greed and its demonic potential to corrupt even the most intimate of human relations.

How does it corrupt? By perverting my sense of identity, from being a matter of who I belong to to being a matter of what belongs to me. Also, by undermining my sense of responsibility, from being a matter of what am I to do for God and my neighbour to being a matter of what I can gain for myself. This is why fasting has been a practice of piety of very long standing in the Judeo-Christian tradition, not least (for Christians) in the period of Lent. Fasting is a symbolic letting go of material things in order to rediscover the primacy of spiritual things. It is the acceptance of 'little deaths' of the self in order to become more alive to God and to God's world. And it is a guard against the spirit of greed and against the idolatry out of which greed springs.

But along with greed, there is something else. Judas is portrayed in both Luke and John as becoming possessed by Satan or the devil. Now, I want to resist the strong temptation felt by many modern Westerners to translate these references to Satan or the devil into a language with which we are more comfortable – to talk in terms of, say, psychological illness instead. Categories like this do not do justice to the reality being referred to. Judas's betrayal has a psychological aspect to it, I am sure. But the Gospels are not all that interested in it. They are interested in giving an account of Judas in relation to God, to the Son of God, and to God's enemy who is identified in personal terms as Satan.

What the story of Judas seeks to express at this level, then, is the awareness that the world is not a neutral place. There is a battle going on between forces which are very much bigger than individual men and women. It is a battle between good and evil, light and darkness, God and Satan. However mythological the language is that we use to express this belief, no other kind of language will do. The reality is too profound and the mystery too great for the language of psychology or history or science or sociology to be adequate. So the Gospels say of Judas simply that

'Satan entered into him' (John 13.27; see also, 13.2; Luke 22.3). Judas, in other words, gets caught up in the battle between God and Satan and becomes an instrument of Satan. We are not told why it is *he* who gets taken over like this, but the idea of his greed may be a clue. It suggests that Judas is more vulnerable to Satan's invasion because his allegiance to God is divided and his moral character is dubious.

There are several warnings in this aspect of the story of Judas. One is a warning about the reality of the invisible struggle going on in the world between good and evil. As the Epistle to the Ephesians puts it: 'Our struggle is not against human foes, but against cosmic powers, against the authorities and potentates of this dark age, against the superhuman forces of evil in the heavenly realms' (Ephesians 6.12). Another is a warning against presumption. Judas is one of the twelve, one of those closest to Jesus, someone in a position of great privilege: and yet it is he whom Satan enlists to carry out the act of betrayal. There is also a warning about the need to be vigilant. In the words of Jesus to the disciples in Gethsemane: 'Stay awake, all of you; and pray that you may be spared the test. The spirit is willing, but the flesh is weak' (Mark 14.38). 'Stay awake and pray' is a good motto for Lent. For that quality of attentiveness and that depth of communion with God are the kinds of skills of the spiritual life which will keep us from falling. And what are we to pray? Surely, the prayer which Jesus teaches the disciples: 'Do not put us to the test, but save us from the evil one' (Matthew 6.13).

There is another important strand in the Judas tradition related to the act of betrayal: it is the theme that Scripture is being fulfilled. A case in point is John 13.18 (see also 17.12): 'I am not speaking about all of you; I know whom I have chosen. But there is a text of scripture that is to be fulfilled, "He who eats bread with me has turned against me." ' This is a quotation from Psalm 41.9 and represents a classic example of Jesus's and the early Christians' sense that the Scriptures are God's living oracles, always relevant to the life of faith, not least in times of testing. Mark and Matthew have Jesus make the more general statement, 'The Son of Man is going the way appointed for him in the scriptures' (Mark 14.21; Matthew 26.24). Matthew also interprets the episode of the thirty pieces of silver as fulfilling Scripture – specifically, of Jeremiah 32.6–15, but also of Zechariah 11.12–13. Finally, Peter's speech about Judas in Acts 1, contains two quotations from the Psalms, the first from Psalm 69.25, the second from Psalm 109.8 (Acts 1.20).

Why is the motif of scriptural fulfilment so prominent in relation to Judas? I do not think that it is a matter merely of finding proof-texts to make sense of something as inexplicable as the betrayal of the master by one of the twelve, though that takes us some distance. It is more profound than that. It has something to do, I think, with the conviction common to 'religions of the book' that life has what we might call an *inscribed* quality. I mean by this the sense that our story is part of a bigger story, and that the contours of that story are found in the Scriptures. Part of a living faith, therefore, involves the two-way process of reading my (our) story in the light of the story of God in Scripture, and of reading Scripture in the light of my (our) story. So when Jesus and subsequently his followers confront Judas, what do the Scriptures enable them (us) to see? That Judas has been with us for a long time. That the person who is righteous will inevitably attract someone like Judas. And that God will vindicate the righteous person and raise him or her up (Psalm 41.10).

It is time to draw to a close, but in doing so, it is worth looking more closely at the dramatic account of Judas's suicide, in Matthew 27.3–10. Although the Revised Standard Version says that Judas '*repented* and brought back the thirty pieces of silver' (27.3), the episode is not about repentance. The verb translated by 'repent' really has the more neutral meaning of 'to change one's mind' (compare 21.29, 32). If Matthew had meant repentance, he would have used a more precise word. In any case, repentance is not likely to issue in an act of self-destruction. At most, then, what Judas does reflects regret or remorse.

But, as Willem van Unnik has shown, there is more to it than deciding on Judas's state of mind.[2] Something much bigger is at stake. It has to do with the social and communal dimensions of sin. What Judas says is very telling: 'I have sinned in betraying innocent blood' (27.4, RSV). In biblical terms, Judas is acknowledging a heinous sin. The shedding of innocent blood is regarded in the Bible as an act of sin which pollutes the land and brings down a curse (see Genesis 9.6; Jeremiah 26.15; 2 Kings 24.3–4; Psalm 106.37–39). Especially relevant to Judas's situation is Deuteronomy 27.25: 'Cursed be he who takes a bribe to slay an innocent person. And all the people shall say, Amen' (RSV). Judas is such a person. He has taken a bribe and betrayed an innocent person. So he has Jesus's innocent blood on his hands and stands under a curse, as ordained by Jewish law. When Judas therefore 'sees' that Jesus is condemned to death, he realizes that he has to act to undo the curse with its polluting effect on the land. So he returns the bribe money, perhaps in the hope that the priests will offer sacrifice for the sin committed. But they dissociate themselves from him. Now, the only option left is for Judas to do away with himself. Only by that means is he able to do away with the curse along with its consequences for the people and the land.

There is food for thought here. Seen against the biblical background I have referred to, Judas's suicide is not a meaningless act. It expresses a recognition of the threat his sin poses to the purity and integrity of the whole moral and social order to which he belongs. And the price he pays expresses the fact that no forgiveness is possible. First of all, the curse has to be removed and Judas himself is that curse.

Here we reach the heart of biblical faith: curse and atonement. The story of Judas is of a sinful man who does away with himself because *he* is the curse. The story of Jesus is of a righteous man who does away with the curse by *being made* a curse for the sake of humankind. As Paul puts it: 'Christ was innocent of sin, and yet for our sake God made him one with human sinfulness, so that in him we might be made one with the righteousness of God' (2 Corinthians 5.21; also Galatians 3.10–14). It is that mystery of curse and atonement that should be the focus of our penitence and thanksgiving during Lent.

3 Love's Labours Lost?

Simon Peter

(Mark 14.66–72)

At the east end of Salisbury Cathedral, there is a most beautiful, modern, stained glass depiction of the passion of Christ, called the Prisoners of Conscience Window. It is by the French artist Gabriel Loire who lives near Chartres, and was unveiled in 1980. I used to live very close to the cathedral, and many times I have sat in the east end chapel meditating on the detail of that special window. There the passion of Christ 2,000 years ago is set between depictions of the passion of prisoners of conscience of today. The detail is such that the closer you look the more you see. So that it was only after several visits that I learned to 'read' a little more clearly the story which the five lancets tell. On the left of the central lancet Jesus is on trial before Pilate. All of a sudden you make out the brilliant red comb and the red and blue plumage of the cock and a small anguished face just to its right: and you know that you are a witness to Peter's denial.

It is to Peter that we turn now and the account of his denial, in Mark 14.66–72, will be our main focus. Of course, there are other episodes about Peter which could engage our attention: being called to be a disciple (Mark 1.16–20), walking to Jesus on the water (Matthew 14.28–32), the confession at Caesarea Philippi of Jesus as the Christ (Mark 8.27–30), or his encounter with the risen

27

Christ by the Sea of Tiberias (John 21) are four good examples from the Gospels, and there are the stories in Acts of Peter the missionary-apostle as well. We will need to keep these other stories in mind. But we are observing Lent, and since Lent is a time for self-examination, a time also for facing our self-deceptions in order that we might love God more truly, then the story of Peter's denial must be where we pay closest attention.

Mark's account of the denial is very dramatic. We will do it most justice if we look at it both long-range and close-up. Taking the long-range view, a strong case can be made that the denial is a culmination of much that comes before it in Mark's Gospel.

The story of the denial is the last episode in which Peter figures in Mark, and it has words and ideas which remind us of the very first. At the beginning of the Gospel, Mark tells us that Jesus comes from Nazareth in Galilee (1.9); he summons Simon and the other fishermen to 'follow' him by the Sea of Galilee; they do so 'immediately'; and they leave everything behind without a second thought (1.16–20). Come now to this last episode. Here, Peter *follows* the arrested Jesus, but at a safe distance in order not to get involved ('from afar', 14.54; compare 15.40); he denies knowledge of Jesus the *Nazarene* (14.67); and he refuses to acknowledge his own identity as a *Galilean* (14.70). Where, at the beginning, he follows 'immediately', now at the end, when he denies Jesus, the cock crows 'immediately' (14.72). Where, at the beginning, he leaves everything for Jesus's sake, now at the end, he loses everything of worth for his own sake. The picture is one of tragic reversal, of so much promise unfulfilled and a brilliant beginning thrown away. To put it another way, we are witnesses of Peter's fall. It is a picture of *love's labours lost*.

The denial also reminds us of the account of the choosing of the twelve, in Mark 3.13–19. There, Jesus chooses the twelve 'to be with him' (3.14, RSV); here, Peter denies being 'with him' (14.67–68, 69–70, 70–71). There, Jesus chooses Simon first, and gives him the new name, Peter (3.16); here, that same Peter denies the name of the one who has named him (14.67). Peter, you see, is denying not just Jesus: he is turning his back on the identity which Jesus has given him and on the group into which Jesus has called him.

Then there is the parable of the sower, given so much prominence by Mark, because understanding this parable is the key to understanding all the parables and therefore the Gospel as a whole (4.1–20, especially vv.10–13). Note the interpretation given to the seed which falls on rocky ground: 'With others the seed falls on rocky ground; as soon as they hear the word, they accept it with joy, but it strikes no root in them; they have no staying-power, and when there is trouble or persecution on account of the word, they quickly lose faith' (4.16–17). This sounds like a precise anticipation of how Peter responds to the threat of persecution on account of Christ, at the Gospel's climax. Yet the fact that he has been taught the parable well in advance of the event makes no difference. He 'immediately' falls. He is unable to endure when the chips are down.

The next relevant episode is the raising of Jairus's twelve-year-old daughter from the dead (5.21–24, 35–43). Peter is one of only three privileged disciples whom Jesus takes into Jairus's house with him, the other two being James and John (5.37). So Peter and the other two are witnesses to the miracle of resurrection. They are shown that death will not have the last word. And this lesson is reinforced for that same privileged trio later when Jesus's divine glory is revealed to them in the transfiguration (9.2–8), and they are taught that the Son of Man is to rise from the dead (9.9–10). The point is this. Peter in particular, and the twelve in general, are given ample demonstration and instruction about the death-defeating power which is at work in Jesus and that he is the one who delivers from trouble (compare 4.35–41; 5.1–20; 6.45–51; 9.14–29). In spite of all this, however, when Peter is in trouble at the story's climax, it is as if all that has gone before counts for nothing. Peter is shown to be utterly perverse and faithless.

But there is more to be seen in this long-range view on the denial. There is also the episode at Caesarea Philippi with the teaching Jesus gives then (8.27–38). Again, Peter is prominent. At first, he shows true insight: 'You are the Messiah', he says to Jesus. But almost immediately, we recognize that Peter's insight is deeply flawed. When Jesus begins to reveal that the Son of Man must suffer, Peter rebukes him and is rebuked in turn by Jesus in the most severe terms: 'Out of my sight, Satan! You think as men think, not as God thinks' (8.32). Peter cannot accept Jesus's understanding of messiahship – that it is a path which leads to salvation, but only by way of the cross. Consequently Peter does not understand what Jesus says about discipleship either, that it also means carrying a cross: 'Anyone who wants to be a follower of mine must renounce self; he must take up his cross and follow me' (8.34). The story of Peter's denial of Jesus later on is the dramatic outworking of the blindness he shows here at Caesarea Philippi. The denial is the Gospel's most eloquent case-study of how hard this lesson about discipleship is to learn, even when the teaching is clear and the person concerned is in a special position.

Then there is Jesus's teaching, amounting to a kind of farewell speech, in Mark 13. It is Jesus's longest uninterrupted speech in Mark and comes just before the passion narrative proper. So it is very important material and is intended to prepare the disciples for the times of stress which start with Jesus's passion. It is significant that the people Jesus is talking to are Peter, James, John and Andrew, precisely the four whom he called to follow him right at the start. To these representative disciples, Jesus gives private instruction in which he warns them that they will be persecuted because of him and exhorts them to be vigilant. Especially noteworthy is the fact that the command to 'watch out' or 'take heed' occurs no less than four times (in vv.5, 9, 23, 33), and that 'keep awake' comes three times right at the climax of the speech (in vv.34, 35, 37). It's a command that points to times ahead, one of which is the time of Peter's testing. The link with what is to come is quite explicit: 'Keep awake, then, for you do not know when the master of the house will come. Evening, or midnight, *cock-crow* or early dawn – if he comes suddenly, do not let him find you asleep' (v.35). Peter's testing comes as the cock crows. That is what Jesus warns about not only here, but also more specifically during the last supper (14.30): and that is what happens (14.72).

I have just mentioned the last supper (14.12–31). Now we are getting very close to the story of the denial. This makes the exchange between Jesus and Peter all the more poignant. Peter, once more the leading disciple and spokesman for the twelve, twice rejects the idea that he will deny Jesus (vv.29, 31). Both of his responses are emphatic: 'Everyone else may lose faith, but I will not'; and, 'Even if I have to die with you, I will never disown you', a statement which, according to Mark, is made 'vehemently'. Peter's words are so strong, so sure, so full of conviction. Not even martyrdom with Christ is too high a price for Peter's loyalty: that is his boast, and it is the boast of his companions too (v.31). But are courageous words and the firmest possible convictions enough? Do Peter's forthright affirmations conceal an underlying uncertainty and fear, perhaps? Or is Peter carried away by the intensity of the table fellowship and the singing of the hymn in the upper room? Will the liturgy translate into life?

The final episode before Jesus's arrest confirms our fears (see 14.32–42). In Gethsemane, Jesus takes with him one more time the trio on whom he depends most – Peter, James and John – and asks them to remain there with him and to watch. But what happens? Three times they fall asleep (vv.37, 40, 41)! And when Jesus is arrested, they and the rest of the disciples run for their lives (14.50).

This is the long-range approach to Peter's denial, in which we have touched on just about all the main references to Peter in Mark's Gospel. But these have not been irrelevant detours. The various episodes are all strands in the same tapestry, or colours in the same portrait. So Peter's denial of Jesus does not come as a surprise. We know in advance that Peter is fallible, just as we know all the disciples are. The denial comes as the prime example of this fallibility. It is the dramatic episode which brings into sharpest focus all that has gone before.

Now we are in a position to move in for a close-up view of the denial. The order in which events are described is important. The denial by Peter is 'sandwiched' between the account of the two trials of Jesus, the first before the Jewish authorities (14.53–65) and the second before the Roman authorities in the person of Pilate (15.1–15). Mark uses this 'sandwich' technique elsewhere: for example, the healing of the woman with the haemorrhage in 5.25–34 is fitted in between the two parts of the story of the healing of Jairus's daughter (5.21–24, 35–43); and the central section with its teaching about discipleship in 8.27–10.45 is sandwiched between two stories of Jesus healing blind men (8.22–26; 10.46–52). This is good story-telling. Its effect is to allow the bracketing stories to illuminate the one sandwiched in between, and *vice versa*.

In the case of the denial, the effect is very striking indeed. For we are presented with a strong contrast: between the trials of Jesus and the 'trial' of Peter. Whereas Jesus stands trial before the whole Sanhedrin and the chief priests on the Jewish side (14.55) and before the governor Pilate on the Roman side (15.1), Peter is tested by an inquisitive maidservant and a few anonymous bystanders (14.66, 69, 70). Where Jesus stands before his accusers and is abused by the guards (14.65; compare 15.16–20), Peter sits comfortably warming himself by the fire in the company of the guards – and we are told twice that Peter is warming himself (14.54, 67). Where Jesus stands his ground in front of his interrogators, Peter is forced fearfully into retreat, from the courtyard back to the gateway (14.66, 68). Where Jesus bears true witness that he is the Christ (14.62; 15.2) and consequently forfeits his life, Peter denies Jesus in an attempt to save his own. Where Jesus remains silent and speaks only what is absolutely necessary (14.61, 62; 15.2, 4, 5), Peter lashes out defensively with denials, curses and oaths (14.68, 70, 71). Where Jesus's silence at the end testifies to his integrity, Peter's breaking down in tears testifies to his ignominy (14.72). The contrast between Jesus and the leader of the twelve could not be greater.

What about other details of the episode itself? To start with, Peter denies Jesus three times (vv.68, 70, 72). So Peter does not just slip up here. His fall is emphatic and unmistakable; and the threefold repetition is part of Mark's story-telling technique, as well as being a characteristic of what Geoffrey Lampe calls 'the whole biblical emphasis on the solemn weight of threefold testimony'.[1] Three times Jesus teaches that the Son of Man must suffer (8.31; 9.31; 10.33); three times in Gethsemane Jesus returns to find Peter and the others asleep; three times Peter denies the Son of Man in his suffering. Peter has not learnt, *cannot* learn, what Jesus is trying to teach and what the Gospel itself is about. It is not coincidental that this pattern recurs elsewhere in traditions about Peter. Acts tells of the triple revelation to Peter at Joppa (Acts 10.9–16); and the Fourth Gospel ends with the threefold commission to Peter to feed Jesus's sheep (John 21.15–17).

Then there is the peril of Peter's position. The irony is heavy here, of course. On the face of it, it is Jesus who is in peril. Mark wants us to know, however, that outward appearances can be deceptive, and that, in this case, it is Peter who is in peril. This is suggested especially in verse 71: 'At this he started to curse, and declared with an oath, "I do no know this man you are talking about." ' The Greek verbs used here for 'to curse' and 'to take an oath' are very strong. Furthermore, although the Revised Standard Version has it that Peter began to curse *himself*, there are grammatical reasons for thinking that we should probably take Mark to mean that Peter begins to curse *Jesus* (compare 1 Corinthians 12.3). If this is so, then Peter has put himself in the position of what other early Christian writers understand as apostasy (compare Hebrews 6.4–8; Galatians 1.8–9). In other words, by cursing Christ and thereby denying his allegiance to Christ, Peter is in danger of cutting himself off from the hope of salvation. Perhaps recognizing this implication, Luke omits mention of Peter's cursing and swearing completely (Luke 22.60). So does John (18.25–27). Nevertheless, earlier on Mark presents Jesus's teaching about the unforgiveable sin of blasphemy against the Holy Spirit (4.28–30) and, arguably, Peter comes close to committing that sin when he denies Jesus. For what he says here is not at all what has been given him by the Holy Spirit (compare 13.11). It is the very opposite, and we are reminded of the words of rebuke to Peter at Caesarea Philippi: 'Out of my sight, *Satan*!' (8.33).

Finally, it is important to note that Peter plays no further part in Mark's story of Jesus. He is not there at the cross. Instead, another Simon has to carry Jesus's cross (15.21), and the only Galilean followers at Golgotha are the women (15.40–41). He does not die with Jesus as he says he will (14.31). Instead, our last visual image of Peter is provided by sombre words which mean something like, 'and breaking down [or dashing out, or throwing himself on the ground] he wept' (14.72). Significantly, perhaps, the only other characters in Mark who weep are the unbelieving mourners at the house of Jairus (5.38, 39).

There is, however, a single ray of hope. It comes, not from Peter, but from Jesus's words to all the disciples at the last supper: 'Nevertheless, after I am raised I shall go ahead of you into Galilee' (14.28). This promise is reiterated by the angel at the empty tomb. To the three women at the tomb, the angel says: 'But go and say to his disciples *and to Peter*: "He is going ahead of you into Galilee: there you will see him as he told you" ' (16.7). That 'and to Peter' is the single ray of hope. Peter does not reappear in person in the story, but his name does, this once. It is as if in spite of the threefold denial, Peter is not cut off from grace (like Judas) after all. Love's labour is not lost. Instead, grace abounds to this chief of sinners, if he is willing to become a follower once again of the one who 'goes ahead' (compare also 10.32) to Galilee and to what 'Galilee' symbolizes – revelation, mission and a new way of life.

Since Lent is a time for self-examination and growth in self-understanding, then the story in Mark of Peter's denial is a valuable place to pause and reflect, long and hard. It helps us to see how easy it is to be a kind of 'fair weather friend' when it comes to believing and obeying God and following Jesus. When the storms come, we sink (see Matthew 14.28–33), when the moment to bear witness arrives, we fall. In modern terms, in the terms of that window in Salisbury Cathedral, it is very hard to be a prisoner of conscience, because the cost is total. It involves, to use another Marcan image, being 'salted with fire' (Mark 9.49), and who is sufficient for that? Certainly, if Peter's story is ours as well, then we will need that 'amazing grace' which comes from the one who goes before us. We will need also to learn those practices and commitments which Peter lacks: prayer, remembrance, discernment, vigilance, endurance, humility, self-knowledge, stability, faith. And we might want to add something also about a sense of humour, which helps keep things in perspective.

It is worth adding that for most of us most of the time, the time of testing when we are most likely to deny Christ will be a passing moment which we hardly notice. Few are called to martyrdom. Only a minority are called to become prisoners of conscience in the literal sense. But all of us face moments of truth which, though they come in the most insignificant of encounters, show whether we belong to Christ or not. As C.S. Lewis says in *The Inner Ring*: 'Over a drink or a cup of coffee, disguised as a triviality and sandwiched between two jokes, from the lips of a man, or woman, whom you have recently been getting to know rather better and whom you hope to know better still – just at the moment when you are most anxious not to appear crude, or naïf, or a prig – the hint [to do evil] will come'.[2]

The prominence of Peter as the leading apostle and (according to Matthew) the 'rock' on which Jesus builds his church (Matthew 16.18–19) allows Peter to function as a symbol of the Church. So I want to suggest that denying Christ is not something done by individuals only. No: it is something to which institutions and societies – even the Church – are prone. Just as in the last chapter we spoke, with reference to Judas's betrayal, of the social and communal dimensions of sin, we need to speak of them again, this time with respect to Peter's denial. The pressure to deny Christ by conforming to worldly values is as much a pressure on the Church as it is on the individual believer. The pressure to deny Christ by acts of institutional violence against people who witness to the truth and expose corruption or against people who just do not fit very well is as much, again, a pressure on the Church as it is the temptation of the individual. The history of the Church is littered with examples of what John Bowker has called 'licensed insanities',[3] where Christ is denied in acts of violence and oppression. This is the testimony of many women. It is the testimony of many blacks. It is the testimony of many poor people. It is the testimony of many lay people, as well. The bleak story of Peter according to Mark speaks directly to the bleak story of the Church. Lent is a time to regard that story with unflinching attention. For true resurrection can come only after a real dying.

But there are those tears. How important they are! Peter *remembers* what Jesus has said, and Peter *weeps*. There is hope here. The act of remembrance is an act of turning to a point of reference in the past which judges and stabilizes and reconstitutes. That is why we observe Lent: in order to remember and recall *our* central point of reference as Christians and as the Church – namely, the passion and resurrection of Christ. And in so doing we are judged and we are reconstituted, brought again from death to life.

4 The Politics of Love
Pontius Pilate

(John 18.28–19.22)

The question whether religion has anything to do with politics, or *ought* to have anything to do with it, is age-old. On one side, there are those who look around them and see the havoc which results when religion becomes a tool of the state or when the state becomes a tool of religion and say that the two must be kept separate. On the other side, there are those who regard such a separation as a sell-out to the forces of secularism and cannot imagine religious commitment as somehow divorced from the affairs of daily life, whether in the home or the workplace or in government and the business of politics. In between, there are those who seek some kind of compromise: religion and the Church have to do with private morality, the family and small-group voluntary activity; but politics is different, as it concerns public affairs, where the specialist skills required are managerial and structural rather than priestly, spiritual and communal.

If I may be personal for a moment, I have long since come to realize that my own formation in this area has been very much of that third kind. What has been of overriding importance has been personal conversion, having a disciplined prayer life and a private life of moral goodness, attending church regularly, and looking forward to heaven or the coming of the kingdom of God (whichever happens first), where 'heaven' and 'the kingdom of God' are understood in rather otherworldly terms and have most to do with the future destiny of the individual soul. And even though I was brought up on the Bible, it was a Bible read in what appears to me now to have been a curiously selective way. What was important was reading it on your own, learning about personal salvation through Christ, and growing in holiness through obedience in matters of morals and lifestyle. A key text was John 3.3 in the Authorized Version: 'Jesus answered and said unto him, "Verily, verily, I say unto thee, Except a man be born again, he cannot see the kingdom of God." ' The primary focus was on individual salvation, holiness and personal assurance, and assurance was safeguarded by a close family life and regular church involvement.

Now, I do not want to deny the good in this. It has its own integrity, I am certain of that; and it captures something of the truth of Christian faith, as many will testify. The trouble is, however, that it does not really have room for politics, management, economics, international affairs, ecology, the workplace, leisure, the arts and sciences, or the public domain in general – except, of course, in so far as these can become areas of evangelistic activity or tools to that end. But there is a more serious failing than this. What I have in mind is the fact that the effective withdrawal from politics and the public domain which is so characteristic of this kind of religion *is itself a political act* (however unwitting), with disastrous consequences. Either it fails to challenge and change the political and social *status quo* or it leaves the public domain open for occupation by forces which may be oppressive and evil.

If there is any truth in what I am saying, then we need next to re-examine the biblical heritage to see whether faith and politics are related after all, and if so, how. I have chosen to concentrate on John's Gospel, partly because it is that Gospel which I have heard so often interpreted in 'spiritual', otherworldly, individualistic terms. Can John be read in any other way? I think it can; and you will not be surprised to learn that we are going to focus our attention in particular on the encounter in John's passion narrative between Jesus and Pontius Pilate.

Before we turn to the account of the trial before Pilate, though, I want to show how important the political dimension is in the Fourth Gospel as a whole. So as in the last chapter, I want to begin with the long view. Of most importance here is John's main concern: to show that Jesus is the Messiah, that is, the Christ. The Jews of Palestine in the first century, were a people under Roman imperial domination, and lived in occupied territory. We know from the writings of the Jewish historian Josephus that, although the emperors recognized the right of the Jews to practise their religion, they also enforced their rule with violence and brutality. They did so through military occupation and by means of their appointed representatives, such as the puppet-kings of the Herodian dynasty and Roman procurators like Pontius Pilate. The latter, in turn, maintained their influence over the people by appointing compliant members of the Jewish aristocracy, like Caiaphas, to the high priesthood. The objectives of Caiaphas and others like him, therefore, were to keep things as they were by going along with Roman domination, even if this meant handing over potential trouble-makers, whether bandits, prophets or messiahs. By collaborating with the Romans in this way, the priestly aristocracy not only protected their own position as the ruling elite. They also preserved relatively intact the identity, religion and way of life of the people of Jerusalem and Judea. I have in here the temple cult along with its calendar and festivals; economic affairs which were tied up with the temple treasury; and internal affairs centred on the meetings of the council (or sanhedrin) and the administration of the Jewish law.

Read against this kind of backdrop, John's Gospel is political dynamite, both in relation to the political outlook of the Jewish people and their aristocratic leadership and in relation to Roman domination itself. Above all, as I have just mentioned, there is John's singleminded focus on the messiahship or kingship of Jesus. John (the Baptist) testifies that he is not the Christ (1.20; also 3.28) but that Jesus is (1.29–34), and he sends his own disciples on to Jesus (1.35ff.). One of these disciples is Andrew who goes and finds his brother Simon and announces, 'We have found the Messiah' (1.41). The next day, Nathanael becomes a follower of Jesus too, with the testimony: 'Rabbi, you are the Son of God! You are the king of Israel!' (1.49). Not many days after this, Jesus goes down to Jerusalem with his disciples and makes an extraordinary and violent demonstration in the temple (2.13–22). Whereas in the Synoptic Gospels this episode comes at the end of Jesus's public ministry, in John it comes at the beginning. So the threat Jesus poses to the temple establishment is clear from the start. It is bad enough that Jesus is a Galilean (1.43, 46; compare 7.41, 52). It is even worse that he should behave in such a dangerous and provocative way in Jerusalem,in the temple itself – and the narrative is heavy already with premonitions of where this will lead: 'His disciples recalled the words of scripture, "Zeal for your house will consume me" ' (2.17, quoting Psalm 69.9).

This Messiah is becoming popular, too. John's disciples follow him (1.35–42). Soon after, the Pharisees hear that Jesus is making more disciples than John (4.1). Then Jesus begins a mission in Samaria, of all places (4.4–42), and there reveals to a Samaritan woman that he is indeed the long-awaited Messiah (4.25–26). As a result of her testimony to Jesus as the Christ (4.29), many from her hometown of Sychar become believers, and testify that 'he is the Saviour of the world' (4.42). What would Tiberius Caesar or his representative, the governor, make of *that* kind of claim, we may ask!

A little later, Jesus miraculously feeds a hungry crowd of 5,000 men and their dependants who have come out to him in the wilderness (6.1–15). Because it happens at Passover (6.4) it is an act reminiscent of Moses feeding the people of Israel in their flight from bondage in Egypt. So does it suggest to the people that they are going to be delivered from bondage to *Rome*? Is it a 'sign' of God's intervention as of old? The answer must be yes, since the people say, 'Surely this must be the Prophet who was to come into the world'; and they are on the verge of making him their king when Jesus withdraws from them to the mountain (6.14–15). The kingship of Jesus is certainly the issue, but in John's telling of the story of Jesus, the question is always, what kind of kingship?

It is a question that comes up again when Jesus enters Jerusalem (12.12–18). Once more, the setting is the feast of Passover, the annual celebration of being set free from slavery to a foreign power. As Jesus comes to the holy city, a great crowd of pilgrims and native inhabitants acclaim him with palm branches: 'Hosannah! Blessed is he who comes in the name of the Lord! Blessed is the King of Israel!' (12.13). There can be no doubting the messianic overtones, nor Jesus's popular appeal: 'all the world has gone after him', say the Pharisees anxiously to one another (12.19). But why the ass (12.14–16)? What kind of king rides in on an ass? What kind of politics is this?

42

Two more points are relevant to this central theme of Jesus's kingship and its political ramifications. First, the miraculous 'signs' which Jesus performs also express his claim to be the Christ, the one authorized and sent by God to give life to a world in bondage and to bring light in the midst of tyranny and darkness. So, many of the people believe in him and say, 'When the Messiah comes, is it likely that he will perform more signs than this man?' (7.31). The sign-miracles are not just acts of individual healing, even though this is how we normally think of them. Their significance is greater than that. They are also political acts which challenge the inherited order and proclaim the dawn of a new order and a new power.

As well as the 'signs', there is also Jesus's sovereign freedom with respect to the Jewish law (or torah). For example, Jesus refuses to rest on the sabbath as is expected of him, but engages in acts of healing. Why? Because 'my Father continues to work, and I must work too' (5.17). Jesus, you see, refuses to be content with things as they are. He is God's Messiah. The old order is important now only in so far as it looks forward and prepares people for the new order which Jesus is inaugurating (5.31–47; 7.14–24; 8.48–59). And Jesus goes out of his way to say – however guardedly, in 'riddles' (10.6) – that the present leaders of the people are corrupt, and that only he is 'the *good* shepherd', where 'shepherd' is a metaphor closely associated with kingship on the model of the great shepherd-king, David (10.1–18).

No wonder, then, that opposition to Jesus grows from a very early stage (see 5.18). Many of his initial followers fall away (6.66). Judas is set to betray him (6.70–71). His brothers do not believe in him (7.5). Above all, the Pharisees, acting in concert with the chief priests, try to arrest him – initially without success (7.32–52), and later in the garden of the Kidron, successfully, with Judas's help (18.1–14). Most telling is a passage which comes at the turning point of the whole Gospel: the raising of Lazarus and its aftermath (11.1–12.50). After the raising, word of the event comes to the Pharisees and the chief priests, the ones most concerned to nip trouble in the bud before it comes to the attention of the Roman overlords. John's account is worth quoting at length: 'Thereupon the chief priests and the Pharisees convened a meeting of the Council. "This man is performing many signs," they said, "and what action are we taking? If we let him go on like this the whole populace will believe in him, and then the Romans will come and sweep away our temple and our nation." But one of them, Caiaphas, who was high priest that year, said, "You have no grasp of the situation at all; you do not realize that it is more to your interest that one man should die for the people, than that the whole nation should be destroyed." ... So from that day on they plotted his death.' (11.47–53). These are the politics of containment and damage limitation, the politics of the lesser of two evils. In terms of what appear to be the realities of the situation, it is perfectly understandable. I guess that most of us would do the same.

We are in a position now to look at Jesus's trial before Pilate. Already we have seen that Jesus is not handed over by the leaders of the Jews in a fit of pique. Rather, it is because he poses a serious threat to the delicate collaboration between the aristocratic priesthood and Roman authority, and so that Jewish privileges under foreign occupation may be preserved. Up to this point, John's Gospel has encouraged us to explore primarily the Jewish side of things, but the encounter with Pilate shows us the Roman side. For the political challenge Jesus presents is

44

not only to his fellow Jews: it is a challenge to Caesar as well. Some commentators have discerned a tendency in the Gospel trial narratives to blame the Jews and exonerate the Romans, but that can hardly be said of the Fourth Gospel. Otherwise it would be inexplicable why John devotes so much space to the trial before Pilate and virtually omits the trial before the Jewish sanhedrin with its formal act of condemnation and the beating of Jesus (compare Mark 14.53–72 and parallels). No, the Roman interest is clearly to the fore. According to John, it is the trial before Pilate which says most about the politics of Jesus.

The story is told with great care, in seven well crafted scenes (18.28–19.16), as Christopher Evans has shown.[1] The first scene (18.28–32) is important. Early in the morning, a time chosen probably to avoid publicity, Jesus is led from the house of the high priest Caiaphas to Pilate's official residence, the praetorium. John tells us that the Jewish leaders did not themselves enter the praetorium so as not to become defiled and be prevented thereby from eating the Passover meal. This is very ironic, because the reader knows that in handing Jesus over they are defiled already. The reader also knows that they are blind to the fact that Jesus himself is God's true Passover lamb (1.29, 36). Pilate asks for the charge on which Jesus is arraigned, and the Jews respond with bluster: 'If he were not a criminal, we would not have brought him before you' (18.30). This is not worth Pilate's time: it is a matter for their law. But now comes the fateful reply: 'We are not allowed to put anyone to death' (18.31). It sounds as if they are trying to avoid responsibility – even though they have been plotting to kill Jesus for a while already (5.18). At the same time, it is an admission of their impotence as leaders of the nation. They are forced to collude with their pagan overlords. In trying to retain control, they reveal their powerlessness.

Now Pilate must become involved. The affair is a capital offence, and a crucifixion – that most brutal and public display of Roman domination – may be in the offing.

This brings us to the second scene, where Pilate confronts Jesus directly for the first time (18.33–38a). It takes place on Pilate's territory, inside the praetorium. At once, Pilate goes unwittingly to what we have seen in the Gospel as a whole is the heart of the matter: 'So you are the king of the Jews?' (18.33). In this typically dramatic one-to-one encounter, the representative of king Caesar confronts another king, himself the envoy of the King of heaven. But Jesus is not at all cowed by Roman authority: 'Is that your own question or have others suggested it to you?', he asks. The interrogator is interrogated himself, and is put on the defensive: 'Am I a Jew?', Pilate responds contemptuously (18.35). There is more irony here. Pilate of course is not a Jew. But at a deeper level, he is one with 'the Jews' in his blindness to the truth about Jesus and the politics of God. And later on, the Jews become one with Pilate and Rome when they acknowledge no other king but Caesar (19.15). From John's point of view, then, neither the Romans nor the Jews are to be exonerated. Both are shown to be blind. Both belong to 'the world'.

But the politics of Jesus, the kingship of Jesus, do not spring from this world. They are of a different order of things altogether: 'My kingdom does not belong to this world. If it did, my followers would be fighting to save me from the clutches of the Jews. My kingdom belongs elsewhere' (18.36). Pilate is mystified. He can think only in literal categories: 'You are a king, then?', he asks, making a stab in the dark. But Jesus refuses to be boxed in by the categories of his opponents: ' " King" is your word. My task is to bear witness to the truth. For this I was born; for this I came into the world, and all who are not deaf to truth listen to my voice' (18.37). In reply, Pilate can do no more than confirm his blindness, his partnership with 'the world'. Contemptuously, he asks, 'What is truth?', unaware all the time that the truth stands embodied before him (14.6). Pilate is so near, and at the same time so far. Because he is not himself 'of the truth', he cannot see that Jesus's kingship *is* his witness to the truth.

Here, we are at the nub of the matter. The politics of the Jews and of Pilate are the politics of domination and subordination backed up by force of arms. They play the same game. It is worth noting that when Jesus is arrested, the party who come for him includes both a detachment of Roman soldiers under the command of a tribune and members of the Jewish high priest's temple guard (18.2, 12). The politics of Jesus, on the other hand, are of a different order of things. When he is arrested, Jesus rebukes Peter for resorting to the sword (18.11), and now, before Pilate, he speaks of a kingship which has no place for the politics of force, because it is not 'of the world' (18.36).

But can we speak of the politics of Jesus only in terms of what they are not? No: I think the Gospel allows us to go further than this. If they are not the politics of force, they are what I think we should call *the politics of love*. In a sense, John's Gospel as a whole is the Gospel of love. The relation of God to the world is one of love (3.16). The relation of the Father to the Son is one of love (3.35; 14.31). The relation between Jesus and his followers is one of love also (14.21). He even calls them his 'friends' (15.13–15) and washes their feet (13.1–20). The 'new commandment' Jesus gives his disciples is to 'love one another; as I have loved you, so you are to love one another' (13.34; 15.12–17). And the response of Jesus to his enemies is one of non-violence. In the powerful metaphor from the lips of John the Baptist, Jesus is 'the Lamb'. Above all, at the

47

end, Jesus demonstrates his love and the Father's love by giving up his life (10.7–18). And when, after the resurrection, Jesus appears to Simon Peter in Galilee, he asks him three times, 'Do you love me?' (21.15, 16, 17).

Of course, this is not a political programme, but it is a kind of politics. It is a very radical kind of politics, as well, because it refuses to play by the normal rules. Instead, it transcends them by calling for a fundamental allegiance to heavenly realities above everything else. And this makes a real difference in practice: Jesus the Jew overcomes a kind of apartheid by speaking to Samaritans, not least a Samaritan woman; he advocates worship 'in spirit and in truth' as being really possible outside temple worship; he reveals in his healing miracles the beginnings of a different approach to health care; he observes the sabbath differently, as a day for continuing the Father's work of creation and restoration; he exchanges power relations of domination and subordination for relations of friendship; he performs acts of religious and political nonconformity in the face of fierce resistance; and so on. The fact that all of this is not laid down as part of a plan and that specific institutions are not developed to carry out that plan may help to explain why Jesus's kind of politics is so unsettling. For it means that every plan and every institution has to be judged according to a new standard: divine love incarnate in Jesus.

In the third, much briefer scene (18.38b–40), we begin to see what happens when the politics of God are rejected and Jesus's witness to the truth is ignored. In spite of Pilate's half-hearted acknowledgment of Jesus's innocence and his probably cynical offer to return 'the king of the Jews' to them, the demand of the people is for the release of another, the 'robber' or 'guerilla', Barabbas. Do we have an ironic pun here? Is John pointing up the perfidy of the Jews by implying that one 'son of the father' (which is what 'Barabbas' means) who is a bandit, is being exchanged for Jesus, the innocent Son of the heavenly Father? In some manuscripts of Matthew's trial narrative there is something similar,[2] where Pilate asks the crowd, 'Which would you like me to release to you – Jesus Barabbas or Jesus called Messiah?' (Matthew 27.17). Clearly, in both Matthew and John, there is a choice, and the Jews choose to reject their own king.

This brings us to the central scene (19.1–3). The politics of violence and state terror move into full swing. Pilate scourges Jesus, even though he has not been formally condemned. Then the soldiers engage in a sadistic mock coronation, with a crown of thorns for his head and a purple robe for his shoulders and mock obeisance. 'Hail, king of the Jews!', they cry; and they strike with their hands the one who himself has no place for coercion and intimidation. And as the violence reaches a climax, so does the irony. Unwittingly, it *is* a king they crown, and a king not only of the Jews. But this is something which the forces of darkness cannot comprehend (see 1.5).

In scene five (19.4–7), the charade continues. Pilate puts Jesus on public display, 'wearing the crown of thorns and the purple cloak'. He protests that Jesus is innocent: but that is part of the charade also. Pilate knows well what he is about. He is humiliating Jesus their 'king' and thereby humiliating the Jews themselves. 'Here is the man!', he says, taunting the people. But the reader knows that, at a deeper level, Jesus *is* 'the man': he is none other than God's Word incarnate (1.14), the Son of Man who bridges heaven and earth and by his death brings salvation (1.51; 3.13–15; 12.23, 34; 13.31). Pilate thinks *he* is in control, but without realizing it he testifies to the central claim of the Gospel of John that Jesus is the true king.

Then, in scene six (19.8–11), there is something of a hitch which puts Pilate in his place a little. On learning that Jesus has claimed to be the Son of God, Pilate becomes suddenly afraid, as if he is aware that he may have overreached himself. So he re-enters the praetorium and talks to Jesus one last time. 'Where have you come from?', he asks. It is exactly the right question, because the reader knows that the origin of Jesus (in heaven, with the Father) is a fundamental clue to his identity and authority (3.3, 8; 7.27–28; 8.14; 9.29–30). But Pilate is blind to that dimension of things, so Jesus remains silent. This provokes Pilate into a petulant tirade: 'Do you refuse to speak to me? Surely you know that I have authority to release you, and authority to crucify you?' And Jesus responds with fearless authority: 'You would have no authority at all over me if it had not been granted you from above'. That phrase, 'from above', is the crux. It signifies the difference between the politics of Pilate and the politics of Jesus: Pilate's politics are legitimate only in the terms of this world; Jesus's politics are justified by an ultimate reality which is referred to simply as 'above'.

This brings us to the final scene of the trial (19.12–16). It is an extraordinary climax, shot through with irony and double meanings. Pilate seeks to release Jesus. He senses, perhaps, that in Jesus, he is dealing with more than he bargained for. But now the man in charge has his own vulnerability revealed, as the Jews (of all people) warn him of the danger of appearing disloyal to Caesar: 'If you let this man go, you are no friend to Caesar; anyone who claims to be a king is opposing Caesar' (19.12). See how the Jews and Pilate depend upon each other! That is what is so grotesque about the politics of domination and subordination. Truth is sacrificed to considerations of mutual survival and mutual advantage. The Jews think it is to their advantage to be rid of their Messiah, Jesus, and use Pilate to that end. It is to Pilate's advantage in his relations both with the Jews and with Caesar to rule as he thinks rulers must, by military might and instruments of torture. So the possibility opened up by the Gospel as a whole of becoming a 'friend' of Jesus and his heavenly Father is sacrificed to the expediency of remaining a 'friend' of Caesar.

So Pilate acquiesces and the show trial proceeds. And once more, Pilate testifies unwittingly to the truth about Jesus. Earlier he has said, 'Here is the man!' (19.5). Now he says, 'Here is your King!' (19.14). But the truth about Jesus is too hard to bear. The light which shines in the darkness is too bright to tolerate. So the Jews cry out, 'Away with him! Away with him! Crucify him!' (19.15). 'Am I to crucify your King?', Pilate asks once more, driving home his advantage. And it is the chief priests, no less, who reply, in words which – for a people who confess only God as king (Daniel 4.32) – amount to an act of apostasy: 'We have no king but Caesar' (19.15). Then Pilate hands Jesus over to be crucified.

The Jews have won, or so they think. They have rid themselves of a messianic troublemaker. But, from the evangelist's point of view, the price they pay is very high indeed. In political terms, their co-operation with Rome has led to an even deeper subordination to Rome. In religious terms, they have given up their allegiance to the King of heaven and his messianic envoy, and the outcome is apostasy: 'We have no king but Caesar'. All this, on the day of Preparation of the Passover (19.14). Instead of celebrating how God had delivered them from foreign domination, they go along even more with their foreign domination by Caesar. Instead of acknowledging the Lamb of God who takes away the sins of the world, they commit the ultimate act of disobedience (19.11) by handing him over to be crucified.

Pilate has won also, or so he thinks. He has maintained and reinforced his (and therefore Rome's) domination. He has repeatedly humiliated the Jews by mocking and humiliating one of their own whom he calls 'the king of the Jews'. He has got another crucifixion, the ultimate testimony to the people's subjugation. And he has shown himself to be Caesar's friend. But from the evangelist's point of view, things look quite different. In judging Jesus, Pilate himself is judged and found wanting. In crucifying an innocent man, Pilate himself becomes guilty of shedding innocent blood. In acting out of self-interest as 'Caesar's friend', he loses any possibility of friendship with a king whose authority is 'from above' and whose rule is universal. This brings us to the final irony. The notice which Pilate writes for the cross of Jesus reads, 'Jesus of Nazareth, King of the Jews', and the writing is in languages which all the world can understand: Hebrew, Latin and Greek (19.19–20). The crucifixion, in other words, is an event of importance for everyone.

In my study at work, I have on my wall a Christian Aid poster with a quite inspirational, close-up picture of Archbishop Desmond Tutu of South Africa. Below the photograph is this quotation: 'I am puzzled about which Bible people are reading when they suggest religion and politics don't mix.' The more I have studied the Bible and thought about my own upbringing and experience, the more I have come to see the truth in what Archbishop Tutu is saying.

The Gospel of John and the story of the trial before Pilate bear serious consideration in terms of the relation between Christianity and politics. For what we have seen, I think, is that being 'born again' or 'born from above'

(3.3) is not a matter of escaping from politics, but of empowerment for a different kind of politics. It is not just a matter of individual salvation but of being personally transformed for witness to the truth. It is not just a matter of private morality but of public testimony by word and action. Above all, it is a matter of receiving power from God to engage with the world in the politics of love.

Lent is a good time to take this challenge to heart. It is a time to see more truthfully *who we are* in the story of the trial. Are we 'the Jews' in our complicity with the powers that be in suppressing the truth and silencing those who bear witness to it? Are we 'Pilate' in the way we enjoy the privileges of power and give in to the demands of the crowd or the interests of our own group? Or are we able to respond to that ever 'new' commandment which Jesus gives to those who believe in him, that we love one another as he, the Good Shepherd, has loved us?

5 The Household of Love
Mary, the Mother of Jesus

(John 19.25–27)

In this next chapter on the people of the passion, we turn to Mary the mother of Jesus. Here I have to begin with an admission and a kind of warning. The admission is that my Evangelical upbringing did not equip me very well with an adequate understanding of the meaning of Mary for Christian thought and practice today. So far as Mary is concerned, I was brought up on what can best be called 'spiritual starvation rations'.[1] In part, this was because the faith I was taught was a faith woven together from texts in the Bible, and the Bible – surprisingly, perhaps, given Mary's significance for Christian identity down the centuries – does not have all that much to say about her. In part as well, it was because the faith I was taught had very little explicit sense of church tradition and the notion that doctrinal truth, including the truth about Mary, takes time to develop. There was also such a strong emphasis on the sufficiency of Christ alone for salvation, that potential rivals like Mary were marginalized completely. Finally, there was a largely unspoken but strongly held consensus that men must have the leading roles, with the result that the women of the Bible, including Mary, were not paid attention; their only function as symbols or role models was as models of self-sacrifice.

So I doubt whether I can do Mary justice. You will have to check any prejudices you find here against your own. You will have to fill in the gaps or perhaps even tell her story quite differently. But a word of warning. There are certain dangers in whatever account we give of Mary. There is the danger of idealizing her in a way which is oppressive rather than life-giving. This can happen, for example, if we so emphasize Mary's virginity that only her sexuality becomes important, and then in a way which can be profoundly unhelpful for both women and men. It can also happen if we overemphasize Mary as mother or wife, since then it is only her relation to significant men which matters, and the only context in which she is relevant is the domestic one. Furthermore, if Mary is set high on a pedestal as that most paradoxical of women, the virgin mother, the danger is that, by representing an unattainable ideal, she will cease to function at all in a life-giving way, catching women instead in an impossible double-bind as they try to attain to both parts of the ideal.

There is some advantage, therefore, in focusing our attention on Mary as she is portrayed in the Gospel of John. For in John, there is no account of Jesus's birth of a virgin, so we are less likely to be distracted by considerations of her sexuality. On the other hand, there is good reason to believe that, as with other characters in John's narrative, Mary is important, not only in her own right, but also as a representative of others. John also gives us two episodes in which Mary figures that are not found in the other Gospels (2.1–12; 19.25–27). The second of these, which depicts Mary standing at the foot of the cross, allows us to include her as one of the people of the passion. Because John is so selective and concentrated in his telling of the story of Jesus, he is more likely to explore the meaning of Mary more intensively than the Synoptic evangelists.

Once again, though, we need to start with the long view. In this case, that means looking at John's overall portrayal of women generally in the context of what he is saying as a whole, before we look at the episodes where Mary features.

Central to the message of the Fourth Gospel is the revelation of Jesus as the incarnate Word of God, the unique Son of God, who comes from the Father to reveal himself to the world as the true and only 'way', and who returns to the Father to prepare a dwelling-place for those who believe in him. The underlying irony of the Gospel is that the people who should believe in him do not, and that those who seem unlikely recipients of revelation believe. The main aim of the Gospel is not just to elicit conversion, but also to confirm believers in the faith they already have (20.30–31): it provides a basis in the story of Jesus for believers to develop their own identity and life together as God's people. John's testimony is universal in scope. It is addressed to women as well as to men. That is why women play an unusually important part in his narrative.

According to John, Jesus the Word of God is the Life as well (1.4; 14.6), the one who gives 'eternal life' (3.16). This means that Jesus brings a new order of creation into being. Just as 'in the beginning . . . all things were made through him' (1.1–3), so now he comes into the world to reveal a new order of things, which is characterized as 'abundant life' (10.10). The implications of this are immense.

On the negative side, it means that the old order is being reinterpreted or displaced. Now, Jesus exclusively is 'the way' to God, not the law as preserved and handed down by 'the fathers'. Now, true worship takes place neither on Mount Gerizim in Samaria nor on Mount Zion in Judea, but 'in spirit and in truth', a secret which Jesus first discloses to a Samaritan woman (4.19–24). Now, the only temple where God is to be encountered is the temple of Jesus's own resurrected body (2.21), encountered first by another woman, Mary Magdalene (20.11–18). In fact, virtually every major symbol of belonging as a Jew (especially a Jewish male) to the people of God – law, temple, festival calendar, sabbath observance, the land, the Scriptures, and the patriarchs – is displaced by Jesus in a way that strikes at the very heart of Jewish norms and culture.

On the positive side, the displacement of the old order of things means that the boundaries marking out the people of God have been redrawn and life as the people of God is to be practised in new ways. Now, there is a new universality: salvation is open to all who believe in Jesus – women as well as men, Greek and Samaritan as well as Jew. In addition, the religion of the patriarchs (see 4.5–6; 8.31–59) gives way to a religion directed by the Spirit (14.16–17, 26; 16.7–15). The life of faith is to be lived according to the utterly demanding, 'new' commandment, 'love one another; as I have loved you' (13.34). That is to say, the practice of the life of faith and the doing of God's will are open equally to women as well as to men in a way which the previous order of things made impossible.

It is hardly surprising that 'eternal life', as revealed by Jesus both in his miracle-working and in his teaching, provokes conflict and division among the people. The coming of a new order of things always generates resistance, especially if it throws into question the identity of a people, their religion, their ways of ordering male-female relations, and their ways of distinguishing insiders from outsiders. In John, the division is felt very keenly indeed. It is expressed right at the beginning, in the prologue:

> The true light which gives light to everyone was even then coming into the world. He was in the world; but the

world, though it owed its being to him, did not recognize him. He came to his own, and his own people would not accept him. But to all who did accept him, to those who put their trust in him, he gave the right to become children of God; born not of human stock, by the physical desire of a human father, but of God (1.9–13).

So people of the new order are called 'children of God', and this distinguishes them, as those whose Father is God and whose birth is a spiritual birth (3.3–8), from those who claim Abraham as their father (8.33) and Moses as their guide (9.28–29). We are witnessing here a real parting of the ways which results, sadly, in a strong mutual animosity (16.1–4). But for the evangelist John, the painful separation is essential, and enormously liberating (8.31–32).

The stories about women express this liberating, counter-cultural faith very well. Notably, the very first of these concerns Jesus and Mary his mother at the wedding in Cana (2.1–12). This episode and the episode at the foot of the cross (19.25–27), frame the entire account of Jesus's mission. They are obviously highly significant for John. But we will return to them, to see them in the light of the other stories about women.

Next, there is the story of the Samaritan woman (4.1–42). Her story is not unrelated to the account of the wedding at Cana. The messianic symbolism of new wine there is reinforced here by the metaphor of living water. The displacement of the cult symbolized at Cana by the filling with wine of the six stone jars used for the Jewish rites of purification (2.6; compare vv.13–22), is reinforced here by the woman's positive response to Jesus's words about true, spiritual worship (4.21–24): she leaves her water jar behind (4.28) to go and tell her fellow citizens about him. And in both episodes, the story hinges on a conversation between Jesus and a woman who shows signs of active faith. By way of contrast, this Samaritan woman shows considerably more faith than Nicodemus, the 'teacher of Israel', in the immediately preceding episode (3.1–12).

The story itself is remarkable. First, we note the pushing back of social and religious boundaries by Jesus: he reveals knowledge of salvation to a Samaritan (4.9, 22), who is also a woman (of some notoriety: vv.17–18). The reaction of the returning male disciples tells all: they 'were astonished to find him talking with a woman' (4.27). Second, what Jesus offers the woman is of inestimable value: liberating knowledge about the nature of true worship and the coming of the messiah. Remarkably, it is here that we find the first of the great 'I am' sayings in John (4.21–26). Third, the woman becomes an evangelist and bears witness to Jesus, with the result that 'many Samaritans of that town came to believe in him because of the woman's testimony' (4.39). Her preaching achieves no less than what the preaching of the male disciples will achieve, according to 17.20. What is more, Jesus's words to the disciples, in 4.35–38, make it clear that her sowing of the seed has prepared the way for their apostolic harvest. In other words, she herself functions as an apostle.

Mary Magdalene is another woman in John's story who has an apostolic role (20.1–2, 11–18). For Paul, according to 1 Corinthians 9.1, an essential qualification for apostleship is to be able to say, 'I have seen the Lord.' It is precisely these words which Mary Magdalene uses when she fulfils Jesus's commission and goes and announces the resurrection of Jesus to his (male) disciples: 'I have seen the Lord' (20.18)! The other disciples say the same thing themselves when bearing witness to Thomas: 'We have seen the Lord' (20.25). This is remarkable. It is as if the evangelist John is wanting to present Mary on a par with the men who are traditionally known as apostles.

Other aspects of the account support this suggestion. For example, John focuses uniquely on Mary Magdalene by saying nothing about the other women at the tomb who are familiar to us from the Synoptic traditions (e.g. Mark 16.1). In addition, the story of Mary encloses the story of the visit to the empty tomb by Peter and the beloved disciple (20.1–2, 3–10, 11–18). So her experience at least parallels theirs, and in one crucial aspect surpasses it, for she is the *first* to see both the angels (20.12–13) and the risen Jesus himself (20.14–18). Then there is the fact that she and the beloved disciple seem to displace Peter. It is they who see and believe (20.8,18), something which is not said of Peter, but which we are left to infer from 20.19–23. Whereas other early tradition claims for Peter the first resurrection appearance (1 Corinthians 15.5; Luke 24.34), John claims this privilege for Mary Magdalene. And Jesus addresses her by name (20.16). For Mary, this is the delightful moment of recognition. She knows now that she is in the presence of the Good Shepherd who 'calls his own sheep by name, and leads them out' (10.3). She is fully a member of the fold: as fully a member as the one whom Jesus calls by the name Cephas, in 1.42. Finally, it is to Mary that the risen Jesus gives the crucial revelation about the nature of his resurrection life: that it is not a matter of mere resuscitation, but of ascension to the Father (20.17). Not without justification, then, has the tradition of the Western Church accorded this Mary the title, 'apostle to the apostles'.

The story of Mary, Martha and their brother Lazarus, in John 11, is another episode where a woman is given a role which other tradition gives to Peter. In Mark's Gospel, a turning point in the narrative is Peter's confession at

Caesarea Philippi: 'You are the Messiah' (Mark 8.29). This episode, so important for all three Synoptic evangelists, is completely remoulded in John (6.66–71). For here, the confession 'You are the Messiah' comes instead from the lips of Martha (11.27). It is to Martha, furthermore, that Jesus first reveals himself as 'the resurrection and the life' (11.25).

This same story is very significant in other respects, too. We note that Mary and Martha, as well as Lazarus, are loved by Jesus (11.3, 5, 11, 33–36). Jesus shows his love for them by raising Lazarus from death: an act which contributes to the loss of his own life (11.8, 45–53), so bearing out his own subsequent teaching, 'There is no greater love than this, that someone should lay down his life for his friends' (15.13). But this love relationship is not just one-way, from Jesus to the family trio. It is a reciprocal love relationship. Mary is introduced right at the outset as the one 'who anointed the Lord with ointment and wiped his feet with her hair': and we are told this before the event has taken place (11.2; 12.1–8). This relationship of reciprocal love conveys the essence of what John means by 'eternal life', and it is shared between women and men alike. As the story of the anointing itself makes clear, such love is costly: it requires identifying with the one who is 'the resurrection and the life' in his death (11.7, 9–11). But it is also full of life-giving fragrance by which the stench of death and of the old order of things is overcome (12.3; compare 11.39).

It is quite clear, therefore, that this evangelist goes further than the others in giving equal prominence to female disciples as to male disciples, including the twelve. This is because, for John, discipleship is not best expressed in power relations which mostly give men the authority for communal affairs. Doubtless, such a development is reflected in other parts of the New Testament, especially the Pastoral Epistles (see, for example, 1 Timothy 2.8–3.13). But John would have viewed this as a backward step into the old order of things, an intolerable compromise with 'the world'. Rather, discipleship according to John is about belonging in love to the new household of women and men who, as 'children of God', 'abide' in Jesus the Son and trust him as 'the way' to the Father.

Now we are in a better position to attend to the two episodes which feature Mary the mother of Jesus. As I said earlier, only John's Gospel has the account of the wedding at Cana (2.1–12) and the episode at the foot of the cross (19.25–27); and the whole narrative of Jesus's ministry is set between these two stories where his mother figures prominently. In fact, the two episodes are mutually reinforcing and in important ways the first serves to prepare the way for the second.

On the surface of it, the wedding at Cana is a simple and rather profane miracle story: Jesus turns gallons upon gallons of water into fine wine! But there is evidently a deeper, symbolic level as the context suggests. This episode comes at the end of a long sequence of testimony to Jesus as the Messiah (1.29, 34, 36, 41, 45, 49, 51). So it would be surprising if this miracle story is not messianic as well: and that is how it turns out, for John tells us that this is the first of the 'signs' by which Jesus makes known his 'glory' – as God's divine agent – and that his disciples believe in him (2.11). What then follows is also significant. Jesus goes to Jerusalem, enters the temple, and violently drives out the traders and money-changers, saying, 'Take them out of here, do not turn my Father's house into a market' (2.13–22, at v.16). This is another action of messianic significance. Whereas at Cana, Jesus miraculously

62

fills with good wine the water jars used for the rites of purification of the old order of things, now in the holy city itself he reclaims the temple itself for God.

But it is not only the context which reveals the symbolic, messianic dimension of the wedding at Cana. There are important features of the content of the story as well. The opening phrase, 'On the third day' (2.1, RSV) is very suggestive of the resurrection (compare 2.19, 22). The wedding banquet is a traditional symbol of the messianic age (Matthew 22.1–10; Luke 14.15–24), as also is the almost ludicrous abundance of wine (2 Baruch 29.5; 1 Enoch 10.19; Matthew 11.19; Luke 7.34). But especially important is the dislocation in the narrative generated by Jesus's reply to his mother when she reports that the wine has run out: 'And Jesus said to her, "O woman, what have you to do with me? My hour has not yet come" ' (2.4, RSV). Such a rebuke hardly makes sense at the level of ordinary human communication between a son and his mother, and comes quite out of the blue. So it is more likely that it makes sense only if the event has a deeper meaning and if Jesus himself has a deeper meaning, as yet hidden from his mother.

The deeper meaning has to do with Jesus's messiahship, as we have seen. For Jesus's messiahship is the only adequate response to the real need, the real 'thirst', of the people which the 'woman' articulates when she says, 'They have no wine' (2.3). More specifically, this episode expresses the claim made explicit later by John the Baptist (in 3.29) that Jesus is the messianic bridegroom come to claim Israel as his spouse. But that extraordinary way of addressing his mother, as 'woman', and that teasingly ambiguous reference to his 'hour' – these are left dangling. In fact, they point forward to the 'hour' of Jesus's death (12.23, 27–33) when the paradoxical truth of Jesus's messiahship is revealed most emphatically, and they prepare the way for the second story where Mary the mother of Jesus features, at the foot of the cross.

In this second episode, Jesus again addresses his mother as 'woman' (19.26); and here too there is a reference to the 'hour' (19.27). But to understand this episode better we need, once more, to consider the context. The preceding account of the crucifixion brings to the fore what we have come to expect: the kingship or messiahship of Jesus. Hence, the notice on the cross, 'Jesus of Nazareth, the King of the Jews', inscribed in Hebrew, Latin and Greek (19.19–20). Then comes the strange account of the division of Jesus's garments by the soldiers, with the casting of lots for the seamless tunic in order not to have to divide it up (19.23–24). That seamless tunic – is it a symbol of the unity of the Church brought into being by the sacrifice of the Messiah? Many have thought so, from the time of the Church Fathers on. Or is it a symbol of the unity of the scattered nation of Israel, gathered into one in this messianic hour when the Messiah lays down his life for the sheep (compare 11.51–52; 18.14)? It is impossible to be certain. What is certain is that this little episode is bound up with what follows, as John makes an implicit contrast between the actions of the four soldiers at the cross, and the presence of the (probably) four women followers (19.25).

This brings us to the heart of the story: 'When Jesus saw his mother, and the disciple whom he loved standing near, he said to his mother, "Woman, behold, your son!" Then he said to the disciple, "Behold your mother!" And from that hour the disciple took her to his own home' (19.26–27, RSV). To understand what John wishes to convey here, we need to note several things. First, if the seamless tunic symbolizes the one people of Israel for whom the Messiah dies, the bringing together of the mother of Jesus and the beloved disciple represents the beginning of the new people of God, the *household of love*. At Jesus's word, the mother of Jesus becomes the 'mother' of the disciple whom Jesus loved and that disciple becomes her 'son' and shows love toward her by 'receiving' her.

Then we may note that at no point in either this episode or the Cana episode is Jesus's mother given her personal name (Mary). She is referred to consistently as 'the mother (of Jesus)', and is addressed by Jesus on each occasion as 'woman'. The effect is to give her a *representative* status, just like the anonymous 'disciple whom Jesus loved'. They represent the new household which the death of Jesus the Messiah brings into being. This new household, this new people of God, has been the goal for which Jesus has come and given his life. That is why John says that 'after this' Jesus knows that the task for which he has come is complete (19.28a; compare v.30).

But how are we to understand John's statement, 'And from that hour the disciple took her to his own home' (19.27b, RSV)? The idea is probably not that he literally takes her into his house to live under the same roof, but that they share henceforth a spiritual kinship as members together of the new household of love. According to Ignace de la Potterie, therefore, a better translation is, 'From that hour the disciple welcomed her into close intimacy'.[2] The allusion is to the Gospel's prologue: 'But to all who did accept [or welcome] him, to those who put their trust in him, he gave the right to become children of God' (1.12). This is the spiritual kinship which the mother of Jesus and the beloved disciple now share by virtue of their identification with Jesus the Messiah in his death. Jesus's death is not defeat. It is life-giving. Raymond Brown puts it well: 'If the Beloved Disciple was the ideal of discipleship, intimately involved with that disciple on an equal plane as part of Jesus' true family was a woman. A woman and a man stood at the foot of the cross as models for Jesus' "own", his true family of disciples.'[3]

Mary the mother of Jesus remains something of a mystery in so far as her personality and individual history are concerned. This remains true even when we try to piece together the various episodes in which she figures in all four Gospels. What John gives us is not Mary as an individual in her own right. He does not even give us *Mary*, someone we might know by her personal name. Instead we have 'the mother of Jesus' who is called 'woman' by her son. She is a representative figure. In John, she represents, together with the pre-eminent disciple loved by Jesus, those who have made the transfer from the household of Israel to the household of the Church bound by the commandment of love. Together, the 'mother' and the 'son' who welcomes her represent the life and faith of the Church which the messianic birth-pangs have made possible. They have shared those birth-pangs by being present at the cross. Now they are bonded together in faith and love as, equally, 'children of God'.

So, even though Mary as a figure of the past may not provide very fertile ground for historical investigation, the Mary of the Gospel of John does provide food for thought this Lent on *discipleship and being the Church*. She reminds us of the importance of what William Vanstone calls 'the stature of waiting' as an important feature of the life of faith.[4] The truth about her son is not immediately accessible to her, but she knows implicitly that there is more to Jesus than meets the eye, and that trust in him ('Do whatever he tells you') will open up a new dimension to life. It will be like the water transformed into the best wine. But she is not ready yet for that. Perhaps she is still too close to Jesus to understand the truth about him. So, interestingly, the Cana story ends by reporting that the *disciples* believed in Jesus: but nothing is said about Jesus's mother, except that she went back to Capernaum with Jesus, his brothers and the disciples (2.12).

Then there is that very long silence, until we come to the scene at the crucifixion, right at the end. But it is a telling silence. It is as if Mary is there all the time waiting and persevering, through all the hard times, for spiritual illumination concerning her son. And this illumination does come, at Golgotha, at the hour of Jesus's death. We know that it is a moment of illumination because the words Jesus uses are words of revelation: '*Behold* your son! . . . *Behold* your mother!' Mary's waiting is rewarded. At the cross, her quest for insight into the identity of her son – at the same time perhaps a quest for understanding about her *own* identity – reaches its goal. And surely, what is true for Mary is true for every would-be disciple. It is at the cross that our quest for the Messiah reaches its goal, and it is there that we are re-made.

These episodes about Mary remind us about something else: that faith and family ties do not necessarily go hand in hand. This point comes through in even sharper form with reference to Jesus's brothers. According to John 7.5, 'even his brothers had no faith in him', and their words to Jesus are full of irony and disdain. The brothers show themselves to belong to 'the world': that order of things set over against God and the Son of God (see 7.6–8). Mary is not like them, certainly. But in order to come to understand Jesus truly, she has to move from the familiarity and prerogatives of her kinship tie with Jesus as his mother to a new kind of belonging in a new kind of household. This transfer takes time and involves the pain of misunderstanding, separation and loss. But through that process, Mary is 'born again', and at the cross she is welcomed into the 'family' of the Church.

Finally, as 'woman', Mary represents a challenge to the Church and at the same time the challenge of the Church to the world. The challenge is that the new way of life which flows from the death of the Messiah is inclusive of women as well as men, and that women as well as men will lead the Church in bearing witness to that life. In saying this, I am reminded again of Salisbury Cathedral. There, some distance from the main north door, is a life-size sculpture of the Madonna, by Elizabeth Frink. Her back is to the cathedral and she is walking away from it. Her body is thin and frail, her face is lined and care-worn, and her piercing eyes are troubled. She bears the pain of the death of her Son. But she goes forward determinedly into the city, there to witness to the suffering of God and the glory of God.

6 Love's Witness

The Disciple whom Jesus Loved

(John 21.15–25)

We looked, in the last chapter, at the portrayal in John's Gospel of the mother of Jesus as one of the people of the passion. She is one of the small group of women who gather near the cross on which Jesus is crucified (John 19.25). But we noticed also that the mother of Jesus is linked in a special way with a male disciple, referred to as 'the disciple whom he [Jesus] loved', and that Jesus's words to them from the cross unite them in a bond of spiritual kinship such that, from then on, the disciple accepts Jesus's mother as his own (19.26–27). Jesus's death is a source of life and brings a new kind of household, a new kind of community, into being. This new kind of community is symbolized by the woman and the man together at the foot of the cross.

In this final study of people of the passion, it is worth lingering over this strange, anonymous and rather characterless figure, identified only as 'the disciple whom Jesus loved'. There may be more to him than meets the eye. It is he, more than likely, who is there at the beginning with Andrew as a follower of John the Baptist, who hears John's testimony about Jesus, 'There is the Lamb of God!', and who becomes one of Jesus's first disciples (1.35–39). Then he reappears in John's passion narrative, at the last supper, where for the first time he is referred to as the disciple beloved of Jesus, and where he has the place of special intimacy with Jesus at the table (13.21ff.). He is there at the cross with Jesus's mother, as we have seen already; and it is probably he who bears witness to having seen the flow of blood and water from Jesus's side which is so significant (19.34–35).

But if he is a privileged witness of Christ's passion, he is a privileged witness of Christ's resurrection also. He it is who runs with Peter to the tomb and finds it empty (apart from the abandoned grave clothes), and of him it is said that 'he saw and believed' (20.2–10, at v.8). Likewise, this same man is one of the seven disciples to whom Jesus appears at the Sea of Tiberias after his resurrection, and it is he who identifies Jesus to Peter (21.1–14, at v.7). Finally, his fate is discussed in a quite remarkable, final conversation between Peter and the risen Lord (21.20–22); and at the end of the Gospel, it turns out that the disciple whom Jesus loved claims himself to be the main author or originator of the work, a claim which the final editor of the work is eager to affirm (21.24–25).

So there are good reasons for taking this figure seriously. He is there at some of the most important points in the story; he is portrayed regularly in tandem with other significant people, like the mother of Jesus and Peter in particular; and he identifies himself (and is identified, in turn) as the author or originator of the Gospel. Above all, he alone of the disciples is designated repeatedly, 'the disciple whom Jesus loved' (see 13.23; 19.26; 20.2; 21.7, 20).

It is at this last point that I want to begin, especially as we are doing our reading and reflecting in the context of Lent. Notice that, as in John's account of the mother of Jesus, this disciple is not referred to by name, even though he is obviously a very important figure. Why is this so? Surprisingly, most modern discussion refers to him as the 'Beloved Disciple' with a capital 'B' and a capital 'D'! Of course, this is intended as a kind of shorthand. But its effect may be misleading, for the tendency then is to concentrate on the identity of the disciple and to ask historical questions like, who in fact was the beloved disciple? The concern of the Gospel, however, lies in a different direction. Its concern is not with the name but with the *relationship*, in particular, the relationship *with Jesus*. So this disciple is not identified by means of a proper noun (a name like 'Beloved Disciple'). Rather, he is identified by means of verbs which show his relationship with Jesus. The first unambiguous reference to him, for instance, describes him thus: 'one of his [Jesus's] disciples, whom Jesus loved, was lying close to the breast of Jesus' (13.23, RSV).

It is hardly coincidental that at the end of John's Gospel, the disciple is referred to again in a way which specifically evokes this first description of him: 'Peter turned and saw following them the disciple whom Jesus loved, who had lain close to his breast at the supper . . .' (21.20, RSV). What is important is not his name, but his relationship with Jesus: he is the object of Jesus's love, and he has the privilege of an intimacy that comes from reclining next to Jesus at the meal table.

Such a portrayal expresses a conviction that lies at the very heart of the Gospel as well as of our observance of Lent, Holy Week and Easter. The conviction is that our true identity as human beings is to be found by recognizing that we are loved by Jesus who as God's representative or 'Son' is the channel of the love of God himself. What is important is not so much, who am I?, or what is my name?, but rather, to whom do I belong? and above all, do I belong to Jesus who is the love of God in human flesh? That is what the Gospel means when it talks about having 'abundant life' or 'eternal life'. For this is the life which consists in being in a relationship of love with Jesus and therefore with God. It is not something we create ourselves, but something we receive as a gift from God through Jesus the Son of God. That is why the disciple we are talking about is described as 'the disciple whom Jesus loved'. In other words, he is passive, a *recipient*. We are not told *why* Jesus loves him. But perhaps that is the point. God's love, God's grace, is like that. It does not depend on who I am or what my name is or what my achievements are. It is just there and freely available. As the evangelist himself puts it: 'God so loved the world that he gave his only Son . . .' (3.16).

We in the West live in a world which focuses enormous attention on the individual. 'There is no such thing as society', some would say, 'only the individual and the family.' Life according to this set of values is primarily about how best to enable individuals to compete effectively against one another in the marketplace. The family then becomes a kind of last bastion of friendship, co-operation and intimate belonging in a heartless world run along other lines. At the same time the family gets caught up in the very consumerism and competitiveness which it is meant to hold at bay. But the Gospel of John is saying something different. It is saying that my value as a person comes not from how well I as an individual compete with other individuals, nor from how well my family performs in providing me with the resources I need, but from receiving God's love made available to me (to us) through Jesus. On this view, I am not primarily an isolated individual, like an atom bouncing around off other atoms. Rather, I am a person loved by God and invited to share in a love relationship with God, with Jesus (the love of God incarnate), and through him, with my fellow human beings.

But it is important to ask what the nature of this love relationship with God and with Jesus is which constitutes 'eternal life'. This takes us back to the disciple whom Jesus loved. He functions in the Gospel as a representative disciple, one who exemplifies what being in a love relationship with Jesus means. The way he is portrayed brings this to the fore. Above all, there is the twice-mentioned close proximity of the disciple to Jesus at the last supper. It is as if the disciple's reclining next to Jesus (literally, 'in the bosom of Jesus') is his hallmark, since reference to this encloses the Gospel's account of him (13.23 and 21.20). This brings to our attention what is so important for the Gospel's understanding of love. Love has to do with remaining close to Jesus, 'abiding in' Jesus, being the friend of Jesus, just as Jesus himself is the one who is 'in the bosom of the Father' (1.18, RSV) and 'abides in' him.

This relationship of love involves at least three things: trustful reciprocity, perseverance, and obedience. The reciprocity is the aspect of response. A love relationship cannot grow and be sustained unless the one who shows love is received with love. In the Gospel as a whole, God shows his love by sending his Son (3.16). At the last supper, Jesus shows the divine love by washing the disciples' feet, a symbolic action which points forward to his subsequent giving of himself in love for the world on the cross (13.1–20). The reciprocity to Jesus's love is of two kinds, represented by Judas on the one hand and by the disciple whom Jesus loved on the other. The two are juxtaposed in a powerful way. Judas has his feet washed along with the others, for Jesus allows no exceptions (13.8). Judas also receives from Jesus the bread dipped in the dish (13.26–27, 30). He shares fully in the hospitality offered by Jesus. But Judas's response is a negative, hostile one: so that when he goes out into the night, the darkness is an entirely appropriate symbol of his position in relation to Jesus (13.30; compare 1.5). The other disciple, however, responds quite differently. He identifies with Jesus by reclining next to him at the table. In this way the Gospel gives us a picture of the disciple's belief in Jesus. Just as later on the disciple 'receives' the mother of Jesus and takes her into his circle (19.27), so here he 'receives' Jesus by taking up this position of intimate association. Whereas Judas severs the love relationship by going out to betray Jesus, the other disciple confirms and reinforces that relationship by staying with Jesus and being alongside him as he looks ahead to his betrayal and passion.

Then there is perseverance. Believing in Jesus is not just a 'one-off' affair. It requires continuing loyalty. That is why John repeats the fact that the disciple whom Jesus loved reclined beside him. His intimacy with Jesus, his love for Jesus, is the same at the end (21.20) as at the beginning (13.23). This impression is strengthened by the references to his presence with Jesus in the turbulent and testing time in between. In all likelihood, it is this disciple who is the 'other disciple' present with Peter in the court-yard, where Jesus is interrogated by the high priest (18.15–16). But, unlike Peter, this 'other disciple' does not deny belonging to Jesus (18.17–18, 25–27). He is present, cer-tainly, at the cross, once again showing a loyalty which is lacking in the other male disciples, for they have gone away (19.25–27; compare 18.8–9). He is present also after the crucifixion, and his perseverance is rewarded, at the empty tomb (20.2–9) and at the Sea of Tiberias (21.7). Indeed, the continuing presence of this disciple is implied or left open as a possibility right up to the very writing of the Gospel itself (21.20–25)! In other words, the Gospel shows us that the love relationship between Jesus and the disciple lasts right to the end. It is not weakened by adversity. It is not shattered by death. For even after Jesus's death, the disciple is portrayed 'following' Jesus (21.20) and 'remaining' perhaps even until Jesus 'comes' (21.23).

Then there is the need for obedience. As Jesus puts it at the last supper, after he has washed the disciples' feet: 'Do you understand what I have done for you? You call me Teacher and Lord, and rightly so, for that is what I am. Then if I your Lord and Teacher, have washed your feet, you also ought to wash one another's feet. I have set you an example: you are to do as I have done for you' (13.12–15). The love relationship with Jesus is not a relationship between equals. Rather, it is something which Jesus initiates by coming from God to give his life in love for the world. As we said earlier, the figure we are looking at is the disciple *whom Jesus loved*. Nor is he the only one. John's Gospel draws attention also to the kinship group of the two sisters Mary and Martha together with their brother Lazarus, of whom it is said that they are Jesus's 'friends', that he loved them, and that (uniquely) he weeps with them (11.3, 5, 11, 33–35).

But the fact that the relationship is not between equals does not make it any less a relationship of love. Modern Western egalitarianism and individualism might find this surprising and uncongenial. That is because many people are sensitive, and rightly so, to the ways in which unequal relationships lead so often to abusive relationships where one person exercises power irresponsibly and destructively over another. But this is not the case in the relationship between Jesus and those whom he loves. There, what is so notable is that the master does not ask his followers to do anything that he has not done already for them. What is so notable also is that his love surpasses theirs. For Jesus is the Good Shepherd who gives his life for the sheep (10.11); Jesus is the one who lays down his life for his friends (15.13). Jesus, in other words, can legitimately ask for obedience in love, because his love for his friends is entirely trustworthy, proven and unstinting – and because it springs from the relationship of love which he shares with the Father and which demands his (Jesus's) own obedience.

The disciple whom Jesus loved is a representative disciple in this aspect of obedience too. Unlike Peter at the end, this other disciple does not need to have Jesus command him three times to feed his sheep (21.15–17), for he is obedient already and has not wavered in that obedience. Nor does he need to heed the command which Jesus gives to Peter, 'Follow me' (21.19), for he is following Jesus still and has not ceased from doing so (21.20). For example, when Jesus on the cross says to this disciple, 'There is your mother', implying that the mother of Jesus is to be the responsibility now of the disciple, he does not hesitate to obey: '*from that moment* the disciple took her into his home' (19.27). He receives her obediently in love because Jesus has received him obediently in love. And that is just one instance of the disciple's obedience. On a wider horizon, we could say that the writing of the Gospel itself is part and parcel of the disciple's obedience to this Jesus with whom he stands in a relationship of love. But we will need to return to this point later.

Now, though, we need to say one more thing about the nature of the love relationship with Jesus which this Gospel explores and into which it invites us. It is something I have hinted at already. This relationship with Jesus is very special, because it is like Jesus's relationship with the Father. Jesus's own teaching to the disciples makes this quite explicit: 'As the Father has loved me, so I have loved you. Dwell in my love. If you heed my commandments, you will dwell in my love, as I have heeded my Father's commandments and dwell in his love' (15.9–10). This bears thinking about. It means that the love relationship which we have from and with Jesus and which constitutes 'eternal life' is, as it were, the 'overflow' of God's love for Jesus. It means also that our relationship with Jesus is guaranteed and exemplified by Jesus's relationship with the Father. We are not left to fend for ourselves.

Nor are we left in doubt as to what 'love' means. For, according to this Gospel, love is what we see embodied, 'enfleshed' in Jesus the Son of God. By extension, love is also what we see embodied in those who belong to Jesus and abide in him. Once again, the beloved disciple is a case in point. He stands in relation to Jesus as Jesus stands in relation to the Father. Jesus the divine Word is 'in the bosom of the Father' (1.18, RSV): this disciple is 'in the bosom of Jesus' (13.23). There is a message of great hope here. God does not keep his love to himself; on the contrary, he reveals himself as love in Jesus. And Jesus reveals himself as love in the people who love him and follow him. So being a disciple at second hand does not matter. The love which was the first hand experience of Jesus's first disciple group is the same love which is available to us through their testimony: 'Those [signs] written here have been recorded in order that . . . you may have life by his name' (20.31).

So far, the figure of the disciple loved by Jesus has helped us to explore what it means to be in a love relationship with Jesus. But there is another aspect of the portrayal of this disciple which is important and particularly relevant for us in Lent. For if Lent is about the remembrance of God's costly love for us made known in Jesus, it is also about learning to bear witness to that love in our own lives and in the life of our communities. That is why we need to

go on in our investigation to show that the special importance of our disciple in the Gospel of John is as *love's
witness*.

The evidence for this is overwhelming. To begin with,
there is the way that the disciple whom Jesus loved is
linked consistently with apostolic figures, most notably
Peter, but also others of the Twelve, as at the last supper
(ch.13) and at the Sea of Tiberias after the discovery of the
empty tomb (ch.21). Since an apostle is understood in the
New Testament and beyond as someone who is a witness
to Christ in his earthly and risen life (e.g. Luke 24.44–49;
Acts 1.6–8, 21–22; 1 Corinthians 9.1; 15.3–9), there can be
no doubt that this disciple is being cast also as a reliable
witness whose authority is apostolic.

Then there is the way he is portrayed. In his first definite
appearance, at the last supper, he alone receives a signal
from Peter to ask Jesus who will betray him; he alone
receives Jesus's reply, which he does not (apparently)
communicate to Peter; and he alone understands Jesus
when he says to Judas, 'Do quickly what you have to do'
(13.27–28). In other words, not only is the disciple reclining beside Jesus cast in the role of a go-between who
interprets Peter's signal and communicates its significance
to Jesus, he is cast also as a unique witness and interpreter
of a crucial element of the Messiah's passion, his betrayal
by Judas.

The same is true in respect of another important detail
of the passion. Alone of the Gospels, the Fourth Gospel
tells of the piercing of Jesus's side and the ensuing flow of
blood and water from the wound (19.34). Then comes the
following statement by the narrator: 'He who saw it has
borne witness – his testimony is true, and he knows that he
tells the truth – that you also may believe' (19.35, RSV).
Who is referred to here? Because the only male disciple

present at the cross is the disciple whom Jesus loved (19.26–27), and because of the determining role this disciple has in the writing of the Gospel as a whole (attested to in 21.24, which itself has strong verbal links with 19.35), we can say with confidence that it is the beloved disciple who testifies to the flow of blood and water from Jesus's side. So once again, he is love's witness. He is able to affirm categorically that Jesus dies and thereby completes the work of love the Father has given him to do. Furthermore, if this same disciple is the anonymous follower of John at the beginning of the Gospel, the disciple who witnesses to John's testimony that Jesus is the sacrificial 'Lamb of God' (1.36; compare also v.29), then his eyewitness testimony at the cross confirms that John's words indeed have been fulfilled: Jesus dies as the true passover lamb, with no bones broken, whose blood is shed to atone for the sins of the world.

Next we come to the accounts of the resurrection. Once again, the disciple whom Jesus loved plays the role of witness – first at the empty tomb (20.2–9), then at the Sea of Tiberias (ch.21). But we can say more than just that. Why is he paired with Peter, and in such a way as to suggest a certain superiority over him? After all, he is the one who outruns Peter and reaches the tomb first, something we are told twice (in 20.4, 8); and he is the one who recognizes first that it is the risen Lord who is calling to them from the seashore and informs Peter (21.7). We are reminded that, at the last supper, Peter has to communicate with Jesus through this same disciple whose relationship with Jesus is more intimate than his.

What does this signify? Not, I think, that the Gospel is attempting to play down the importance of Peter. The point, rather, is a positive one. It is, as Richard Bauckham has shown, that the witness of the disciple whom Jesus loved is 'a *perceptive* witness, with spiritual insight into the meaning of the events of the Gospel story'.[1] In other words, it is not just that he is a witness – since almost every character in the Gospel, including Peter, functions as a witness to Jesus in some way or other – but that he is a witness of particular insight. This implies, in turn, that his witness is authoritative and reliable. And he is reliable, not only as a witness, but as an *interpreter* of what he sees, as well. This helps make sense of the statement that when the disciple went into the empty tomb after Peter, it is he – that is, he not Peter, or he more than Peter, or he before Peter – who 'saw and believed' (20.8). Likewise, on the Sea of Tiberias, there is Peter's curious dependence on the beloved disciple for the true interpretation of what they both see and hear: '*As soon as Simon Peter heard him say*, "It is the Lord", he fastened his coat about him . . . and plunged into the sea' (21.7).

But we must ask now the obvious question: what is it about this disciple which makes him the supremely reliable witness and perceptive interpreter? The answer, I think, flows from what we were considering earlier: the relationship of love between the disciple and Jesus. It is not just that the disciple is there at the crucial events, although that is important, especially when others are absent. More than that is involved. The Gospel account invites us to recognize that the insight, perceptiveness and sensitivity of the disciple arise out of the love which he has for and receives from Jesus. The disciple whom Jesus loved is more clearly in tune with the meaning of the events of Jesus's life and passion and more sensitive to the presence of Jesus in the period after the passion because he is in that trustful, abiding and obedient relationship of love with the one who is Love incarnate. Just as the Son is loved by the Father and witnesses to that love with unsurpassed authority and fidelity, so the beloved disciple is loved by Jesus and becomes himself love's witness. Raymond Brown makes the point in a similar way when he says: 'Faith is possible for the Beloved Disciple because he has become very sensitive to Jesus through love. . . . The lesson for the reader is that love for Jesus gives one the insight to detect his presence. The Beloved Disciple, here as elsewhere the ideal follower of Jesus, sets an example for all others who would follow.'[2]

There is one final issue worth considering. It concerns the form this witness to Jesus takes. Here, the pairing of the disciple with Peter is significant once again, especially as it occurs in John 21. If we ask what is the form of witness which arises out of the relationship of love which *Peter* has with Jesus, the clear answer from Jesus's threefold command to him is that Peter is to take over Jesus's own role as shepherd of the sheep (see 21.15–17). Peter is to become the active leader of Jesus's followers once the Good Shepherd has departed. This active leadership is implied already in the portrayal of Peter, not least in this final episode, which shows Peter jumping into the sea to go to Jesus (21.7–8), returning to the boat to bring the net full of fish to land (21.10–11), and later on putting to Jesus the question about the fate of the beloved disciple (21.20–22).

If then Peter's witness is to take the form of active leadership of the community of followers, what kind of witness will be that of the disciple who is paired with him? The answer is embodied in the Gospel text itself. This authoritative and sensitive putting-into-words of the Word made flesh is itself the witness of the disciple whom Jesus loved. That is how we should understand the penultimate verse of the whole Gospel: 'It is this same disciple [whom Jesus loved] who vouches for what has been written here. He it is who wrote it . . .' (21.24). Not for him the way of active leadership which is the kind of witness Peter is to exercise, but rather the way of faithful, perceptive and inspired handing on of tradition as a witness which is equally as important as that of Peter. The one cannot do without the other. Without the inspired guidance of the trustworthy interpreter of the tradition, Peter's leadership and the work of those he leads will degenerate into shallow activism. Without Peter's leadership, there will be no continuing community to embody and practise the truth of the tradition mediated to it by the beloved disciple.

This is a good place to bring our reflections on people of the passion to a close. For we have come to the point of recognizing that it is possible to speak of two ways of responding to the passion of Christ, two ways of witnessing to the love of God in Christ, two types of spirituality. Peter represents the way of action, the beloved disciple represents the way of meditation. Peter represents the way of planning and rational decision-making, as when he asks Jesus, 'Lord, what about him?' (21.21), or as earlier, when he signals to the disciple next to Jesus to ask which of the disciples is to betray him (13.24). The beloved disciple represents the way of intuition, receptivity and imagination which is expressed so profoundly in his writing. Peter represents the extrovert, heroic kind of spirituality which thrives on overcoming opposition and hardship, and which is the stuff of martyrdom: hence Jesus's prophecy of how Peter is to die, in 21.18–19. The beloved disciple represents a more introvert, unobtrusive, long-suffering kind of spirituality. The end of such a disciple or community may be less dramatic (21.23), but it is by no means less faithful.

Both of these are valid ways of responding, this and every Lent, to the passion of Christ. The one does not exclude the other. Indeed, Lent may be a time when we come to recognize that we have been too much of one and not enough of the other. So there is the invitation. Jesus asks that simple, direct question, 'Do you love me?' And he wants us to respond by acts of love to those for whom he has given his life. But such acts will be shallow or misdirected unless they are guided and nurtured by being in a relationship of love with Jesus. We can respond properly to the question 'Do you love me?' only when we have come to see that we are loved already.

NOTES

Chapter 1

1. C.E.B. Cranfield, *The Gospel According to St. Mark* (Cambridge University Press 1963, revised edn), p. 415

Chapter 2

1. Bertil Gärtner, *Iscariot* (Fortress 1971), p.18
2. See W.C. van Unnik, 'The Death of Judas in Saint Matthew's Gospel', *Anglican Theological Review,* Suplementary Series No. 3, March 1974, pp.44–57

Chapter 3

1. G.W.H. Lampe, 'St. Peter's Denial', *Bulletin of the John Rylands Library*, 55, 1972–73, p.352
2. C.S.Lewis, *Screwtape Proposes a Toast* (Collins 1965), pp.36–37
3. John Bowker, *Licensed Insanities: Religions and Belief in God in the Contemporary World* (DLT 1987)

Chapter 4

1. See C.F. Evans, *Explorations in Theology 2* (SCM 1977), pp.50–66
2. For comment on the relevant Caesarean text, see B.M. Metzger, *A Textual Commentary on the Greek New Testament* (United Bible Societies 1971), pp.67–68

Chapter 5

1. See Ann Loades, 'The Virgin Mary and the Feminist Quest', in J.M. Soskice, ed., *After Eve* (Marshall Pickering 1990), p.162
2. Ignace de la Potterie, *The Hour of Jesus* (St. Paul 1989), p.149
3. R.E. Brown, *Community of the Beloved Disciple* (Geoffrey Chapman 1979), p.197
4. W.H. Vanstone, *The Stature of Waiting* (DLT 1982)

Chapter 6

1. R. Bauckham, 'The Beloved Disciple as Ideal Author', *Journal for the Study of the New Testament*, 49, 1993, p.37
2. R.E. Brown, *The Gospel According to John XIII–XXI* (Geoffrey Chapman 1972), p.1005

FURTHER READING

Chapter 1

S.C. Barton, 'Mark as Narrative. The Story of the Anointing Woman', *Expository Times*, 102/8, 1991, pp.230–34

E.S. Fiorenza, *In Memory of Her* (SCM 1983)

J.A. Grassi, *The Hidden Heroes of the Gospels: Female Counterparts of Jesus* (Liturgical Press 1979)

E.S. Malbon, 'Fallible Followers: Women and Men in the Gospel of Mark', *SEMEIA*, 28, 1983, pp.29–48

D. Rhoads and D. Michie, *Mark as Story* (Fortress 1982)

Chapter 2

B. Gärtner, *Iscariot* (Fortress 1971)

W. Klassen, 'Judas Iscariot', *The Anchor Bible Dictionary*, 3 (Doubleday 1992), pp.1091–96

H. Maccoby, *Judas Iscariot and the Myth of Jewish Evil* (Peter Halban 1992)

F.J. Matera, *Passion Narratives and Gospel Theologies* (Paulist 1986)

I. de la Potterie, *The Hour of Jesus* (St. Paul 1989)

D. Senior, 'A Case Study in Matthean Creativity', *Biblical Research*, XIX, 1974, pp.23–36

W.C. van Unnik, 'The Death of Jesus in Saint Matthew's Gospel', *Anglican Theological Review,* Suplementary Series No. 3, March 1974, pp.44–57

W.H. Vanstone, *The Stature of Waiting* (DLT 1982)

Chapter 3

S.C. Barton, *The Spirituality of the Gospels* (SPCK 1992), pp.39–70

R.E. Brown *et al.*, eds, *Peter in the New Testament* (Paulist 1973)

O. Cullmann, *Peter Disciple Apostle Martyr* (SCM 1962)

S. Freyne, *Galilee, Jesus and the Gospels* (Gill and Macmillan 1988), pp.33–68

G.W.H. Lampe, 'St. Peter's Denial', *Bulletin of the John Rylands Library*, 55, 1972–73, pp.346–68

F.J. Matera, *Passion Narratives and Gospel Theologies* (Paulist 1986)

H. Merkel, 'Peter's Curse', in E. Bammel, ed., *The Trial of Jesus* (SCM 1970), pp.66–71

Chapter 4

C.F. Evans, *Explorations in Theology 2* (SCM 1977), pp.50–66

F. Millar, 'Reflections on the Trials of Jesus', in P.R. Davies and R.T. White, eds., *A Tribute to Geza Vermes* (JSOT 1990), pp.355–81

D. Rensberger, *Johannine Faith and Liberating Community* (Westminster 1988), pp.87–106

E. Rivkin, *What Crucified Jesus?* (SCM 1986)

E. Schürer, *The History of the Jewish People in the Age of Jesus Christ*, Vol. I, rev. edn, (T&T Clark 1973), pp.383–87

H. Schlier, 'The State according to the New Testament', in *The Relevance of the New Testament* (Herder and Herder 1968), pp.215–38

A.N. Sherwin-White, *Roman Society and Roman Law in the New Testament* (Clarendon 1963), pp.24–47

Chapter 5

S.C. Barton, 'Women, Jesus and the Gospels', in R. Holloway, ed., *Who Needs Feminism?* (SPCK 1991), pp.32–58

R.E. Brown *et al.*, *Mary in the New Testament* (Fortress 1978)

R.E. Brown, *The Community of the Beloved Disciple* (Chapman 1979)

I. Gebara and M.C. Bingemer, *Mary, Mother of God, Mother of the Poor* (Burns & Oates 1989)

A. Loades, 'The Virgin Mary and the Feminist Quest', in J.M. Soskice, ed., *After Eve* (Marshall Pickering 1990), pp.156–78

I. de la Potterie, *The Hour of Jesus* (St. Paul 1989)

M. Warner, *Alone of All Her Sex* (Quartet 1978)

Chapter 6

R. Bauckham, 'The Beloved Disciple as Ideal Author', *Journal for the Study of the New Testament*, 49, 1993, pp.21–44

R.F. Collins, 'The Representative Figures of the Fourth Gospel – II', *Downside Review*, 94, 1976, pp.118–32

R.A. Culpepper, *Anatomy of the Fourth Gospel* (Fortress 1983)

M. Davies, *Rhetoric and Reference in the Fourth Gospel* (Sheffield
    Academic 1992), pp.340–47
M. Hengel, *The Johannine Question* (SCM 1989)

Also by Stephen Barton

THE SPIRITUALITY OF THE GOSPELS

The aim of this book is to help today's readers to explore what each Gospel has to offer when viewed in its own right as a classic of Western spirituality. Written in a clear, non-technical style, the fresh perspectives it presents will open new vistas on prayer and the life of faith drawn from the familiar stories about the life, teaching, passion and resurrection of Jesus.

Published by SPCK

Tri∧ngle and SPCK
Books
can be obtained from
all good bookshops.
In case of difficulty,
or for a complete list of our books,
contact:
SPCK Mail Order
36 Steep Hill
Lincoln
LN2 1LU
(tel. 0522 527 486)